Remember Me

For Beverly
Family Stories

Peter B Stipe

Peter Stipe

Aster Press
An imprint of Blue Fortune Enterprises, LLC

REMEMBER ME
Copyright © 2018 by Peter Stipe.

This book is a work of fiction. Names, characters, businesses, organizations, places, events and incidents either are the product of the author's imagination or are used fictitiously. Any resemblance to actual persons, living or dead, events, or locales is entirely coincidental.

For information contact :
Blue Fortune Enterprises, LLC
Aster Press
P.O. Box 554
Yorktown, VA 23690
http://blue-fortune.com

Book and Cover design by Wesley Miller, WAMCreate, wamcreate.co

ISBN: 978-1-948979-10-8
First Edition: November 2018

DEDICATION

For my mother, Elma MacMurray Stipe
and for her father, James H. MacMurray
and for his parents, Oscar and Maggie McMurray.
This is their story.

Table of Contents

Foreword

I DON'T KNOW WHO I am or where I come from. I know little about my family history and I have met very few of my relatives. My mother made occasional references throughout my life to some distant relatives, Oscar and Maggie—Margaret, as my mother called her. Mother told me they were my great-grandparents, but she shared scant details about them. Family history was not a topic she liked to discuss.

We are not a family who preserves keepsakes from our ancestors, but my mother was a pack rat who never threw anything away. Keeping things is not the same as preserving them along with the accompanying stories about their significance. There have always been a few odd items lying around. I now know that some of these belonged to Oscar McMurray and his wife Maggie.

I have always been intrigued with these heirlooms. Today I am sitting in my office to write, surrounded by these keepsakes and relics. They inspire me. They have been passed down to me, but I know little about most of them. Who made them? How did they come into my possession?

I work every day at my father's writing desk. I know the story behind the desk because it begins within my lifetime. It's an antique, with carved wooden legs, inlays of whorled wood, etched with flower and leaf patterns, a design suggesting it was probably made during the second half of the nineteenth century, but it has no family history. My father found it in a used furniture store and, being a practical man who needed a desk, he saw it as a functional addition to his office. Late in my father's life, when he was no longer working, he gave it to me for my home office, knowing that I liked the look of the old desk. I cleaned it up, restored it, gave it a new dark brown leather top and started on my writing. I have my computer with a blue-tooth keypad and mouse on it, totally anachronistic.

The heirlooms that have been passed down to me are harder to explain. There should be stories with each of them, explaining how our family came to own them and where they fit into our heritage. I want to know these folktales. My family history matters to me. I need to know about my ancestors, the people who created the family I was born into.

I have discovered that my mother's account of Oscar and Maggie's lives was not accurate. Whether this deception began with her father James MacMurray or started with my mother herself is unclear. As I researched my mother's stories, I began to unravel the truth about my ancestors, about Oscar and Maggie and their relatives. I now imagine what their lives might have been like based on what I discovered.

Every family has its stories, an oral history passed down from parents to their children that ties the generations together, connecting today's children to their past. The legends change over the years. They are embellished; details are added or forgotten. I never realized family stories were commonplace until I was an adult and had moved out on my own. When I met the families of my friends, I found that many of them had a rich tradition of family folklore. These are the tales shared around the table at family gatherings, laughed about through the generations. My wife Debbie's family has a long history of sharing their stories. I don't have this heritage. I wonder today why I lack these accounts, these traditional family tales.

My father, J. Gordon Stipe Jr., was a college professor, an introverted man who spent much of his time at home behind the closed door of his study, working on a textbook he was writing or preparing for his classes. His mother had died when he was a boy. His father was a Dean at Emory University who visited our house only once when I was still young. He died a year or two later. I hardly remember him. My father rarely told family stories, so I know little about the Stipe side of my family.

My mother, Elma MacMurray Stipe, was also reluctant to talk about her family history. She had a very close relationship with her father, James MacMurray, but he died while she was in college. Her mother, Grace Cooper MacMurray, lived much longer. She was still alive when Debbie and I got married. She is the only grandparent I really knew. There were a few distant aunts and uncles on my mother's side of the family, but they too shared little information about our history.

It is unfortunate that neither my mother nor my father said much about their family history or cherished the keepsakes that have been passed down to me. Sometimes the lack of stories was negligence; they didn't seem to matter to my parents, so they let them die. Too often, our family tradition has been to wipe out the past, to obscure the oral traditions, a deliberate act, erasing our history. I don't know why this happened, but it means we have lost our heritage. That concerns me. In recent years I have begun to dig into my family history seeking answers, trying to explain these heirlooms, hoping to learn about my ancestors.

I never would have created this account of the lives of Oscar and Maggie if my mother hadn't told me so much about them that wasn't true, if her story of their lives had been more complete, more accurate — based on facts. But it has turned out that what she told me about their lives doesn't match what I learned from my research. I want to understand my family history. If my mother's stories aren't accurate, shouldn't I write a new story based on the facts, a family story that might be true?

It distresses me that the story of Oscar and Maggie's life together has been lost. I don't want them to be forgotten. I need to know who they were and to preserve their lives as best I can.

The Family Tree

Robert J. McMurray born 10/17/1798
died in Albany - 6/18/1846
married c. 1818? **Abigail Spicer** 7/26/1798 – 10/11/1853

James H. McMurray
born 3/4/1819 Lansingburgh, NY
died 12/9/1888 St. Paul, Minnesota
married
5/2/1841 **Hannah Otis** in Lansingburgh
born 1822 St. John's Canada
died 6/27/1866 in Lansingburgh
married **Sarah Otis** 10/15/1867 in
Columbus, OH. Moved to St. Paul, MN
Sarah was born 2/10/1830 in Canada

Albert born before 1825. Date unknown
Possibly 2 children: Clarence? Ada?
Charlotte born 1825
George born 1833. Married **Mary
Sylvester (Stub)** born 6/17/1837 in
Lansingburgh – died 3/25/1916 in
Argyle, NY
Stub married **Ann Lovinia McIntyre**
1/16/1868
Ann Mcintyre McMurray 1842 - 6/xx/1925
Adelaide born x/x/1843
Addie married Royal "Rollo" Comstock
9/28/1865 in Lansingburgh.

Oscar E. McMurray born 8/27/1843
in Lansingburgh. died 2/2/1907 in
Vailsburg, NJ
Anna Maria 7/25/1845 – 1/24/1852
Eugene A. 10/12/1847 – 5/31/1868 in
OH
Paolina P. 7/6/1850 – 8/21/1852
Sarah Emma 7/17/1852 – 10/4/1927
in OH
Anna Maria II 7/25/1854 - 1913

Oscar marries **Margaret J. Teachout**
4/4/1867 in Waterford, NY
Margaret Jane Teachout McMurray
Born 5/25/1848 in Waterford
Died 12/11/1921 Vailsburg, NJ

James H. MacMurray married **Grace
E. Cooper,** 5/29/1920 in Maplewood, NJ
Grace C. MacMurray born 1889, died
April, 1976

Carrie M. McMurray born 5/13/1868.
died 1951. Never married
Eugene A. McMurray born 5/8/1872.
married **Mabel Apgar** 5/10/1904 in
Germantown, NJ
Divorced in 1925. Remarried Bessie
Lambright
James H. MacMurray born 8/29/1875.
died 8/15/1940 in Maplewood, NJ
Edna J. McMurray born 6/6/1891.
died 2/29/1892 in Newark, NJ

Elma MacMurray born 4/7/1921
Maplewood, NJ. died 8/6/2015 in
Southborough, MA. married in
Maplewood, 3/13/1943 to **J. Gordon
Stipe Jr.** born 1/1/1914 Decatur, GA.
died 3/17/1988 in Southborough, MA

Grace-Anne Stipe Benoudiba born
1945 in Princeton, NJ. married **Victor
Benoudiba,** December, 1972. Now
lives in Biarritz, France.

Peter Gordon Stipe born 1947 in PA.
married **Debra LaOna Carr,** 1974.
Now lives in Williamsburg, VA

Tina Benoudiba, born 1973
Daniel Benoudiba, born 1976

David Gordon Stipe, born 1980
Carey LaOna Stipe, born 1983

1

How It Ended

I HAD BEEN WRITING fiction for years, and shortly after I retired and moved to Virginia I found a publisher who agreed to publish a collection of my short stories. It was a wonderful moment for me, my first book accepted for publication, another of my life goals achieved. My mother became angry when she learned that I was getting a book published. She had also done some writing years ago when I was a child. None of her writing had been published, and she believed it was wrong that I had succeeded with one of her personal goals when she had been unsuccessful.

She was upset by so many things I had done, and angry about other things I had not done, things that were her dreams for me. My dreams and aspirations were different than those my mom had for me. Today I am content with what I have accomplished in my life. I have attained some of my goals. I have fallen short with others but either way, the successes and near misses are mine. My move to Virginia to be close to where my children lived was the most recent disappointment for her. She hated the time we had lived in Virginia during my childhood.

When my book of short stories was almost ready for publication, on a Monday in early August, I met my publisher for lunch. She gave me a proof copy of my book. The rounds of editing were complete, and the cover artwork was set. All I needed to do was take a final look through the book, noting any last changes, and the book would go to press. I called Mother that Monday evening and told her my good news. She changed the subject. She was still upset that I was getting published when she hadn't.

On Wednesday morning I finished the final review of my book and sent my publisher a few last corrections. We were set. My book was ready.

I leaned back in my chair at my desk, remembering the moment two days earlier when I first held that proof copy of my book. I was as proud as a new daddy holding his first-born child. For a moment I cried with joy. Now the book was finally on its way and I couldn't wait.

My cell phone buzzed, ending my daydreaming. It was Joyce, my mother's neighbor in Massachusetts. "Peter? Your mom is ill. She's not doing well. I found her this morning when I came to see her. Each morning I pick up her newspaper at the end of the driveway and look in on her. Today she's having trouble."

"Could I speak with her?"

Joyce handed her phone to my mother. "Mom? How are you feeling?" I asked.

"Okay." Her voice was weak, emotionless.

"Joyce told me you're not feeling well."

"No. I've been having some indigestion the last few days."

"Are you in pain? Have you gotten up from bed today?" It was nearly noon. Mother had always believed it was sinful to sleep late, wasting the day.

"No, I'm still in bed," mother replied with irritation, maybe anger touching her voice. To her, to be sick was a sign of weakness. We were supposed to be stronger than that. She sighed and added, "Yes, there's a lot of pain."

"Do you think you should see the doctor?" Mother hated doctors and hospitals. Both my dad and my stepdad died of cancer, and she believed they could have been saved if they hadn't been taken to hospitals "where they take people to die." I hoped she wouldn't rule out a visit to a doctor when she clearly needed help.

To my surprise she answered, "Yes. They should probably take me to a hospital so they can do something about how I'm feeling."

I stayed on Joyce's phone with Mother. Joyce called the EMTs on Mom's phone and remained with her until they arrived. I could hear the EMTs as they checked on her. Again, I was shocked to hear her tell them, "I should probably go to the hospital. Could you get me to the hospital in Framingham?" It had to be bad if she was asking to go to the hospital.

I talked with Joyce again and listened as the EMTs prepared to get Mother out to the ambulance. Then Joyce hung up, and I was alone at my writing table. Debbie was out grocery shopping. I texted her that Mother was in trouble, and she needed to hurry home. When she got home, we discussed the situation over a quick lunch and packed our bags for the trip north, expecting to be with my mother for perhaps a week until she was stabilized. It was more than a ten-hour drive from our Virginia home to her house in Massachusetts. We were on the road later that afternoon.

I was Mother's medical proxy, authorized to answer for her when she was unable to speak. A doctor had been in contact that evening as we drove, asking permission to operate, to explore and find the cause of her pain. I agreed. That he didn't call back later that night after the surgery was good news. She was still alive. We spent a restless night in a motel in Delaware, waking often, dreading that the phone would ring with bad news. We were back on the road by dawn. We talked again with Joyce and notified friends in Massachusetts of our situation. We received offers from friends of homes where we could stay during Mother's hospitalization.

We got to the hospital by mid-afternoon and were directed to my mother's room in Intensive Care. I was stunned to walk in and see Mother sleeping in a bed with tubes in her arms and a ventilator connected to her mouth and nose. My nephew Daniel lived and worked nearby and was already there with his wife Anne. Daniel stood at the end of her bed. He had been crying, and Anne held him with an arm around his shoulders.

"How is she?" I asked, seeing that things were bad, but hoping for a word of encouragement from Daniel or Anne.

"Not good," Daniel said. His voice choked. Anne held him tighter. My sister had moved to France decades ago. Daniel is her second child and a dual citizen, able to travel easily between France and the States. Ten years earlier he had come back to the United States in search of a job. He had established a nice career for himself and married a wonderful woman from the town where I used to teach high school. But dealing with death was new for him. He fought to hold himself together.

A nurse brought in the surgeon. He led all of us to a small, quiet room next to the ICU. The room was comfortable, outfitted like a living room with couches and chairs, potted plants and a coffee table with copies of People magazine and Sports Illustrated. He gave us the hard news that Mother had an intestinal infection that had turned bad. Her intestine had ruptured, and her body was filled with the infection. He had stitched up the intestine as best he could, but she was too weak to fight the infection. She was depending on life support and pain-killers to stay alive.

"What's the prognosis?" I asked. "Will she make it?"

The doctor answered calmly but with compassion. "No. I could operate again to see if I can fix her completely inside. But she's ninety-four years old, and right now she's so weak that I doubt if she would survive a second surgery."

"How long does she have?"

"Her body has turned toxic. If we keep her connected to life support, she might last at best several days, maybe a week. Probably much less."

"And if we disconnect her?"

"Less than an hour."

"Is she in pain?"

"No. She's in a coma and on medication to mask the pain, but even on life support she's fading fast. She might not last the night."

"Does she know we're here?"

"It's hard to say. Some people believe that yes, even in a coma she would know. But she's unable to respond. It's better that you're all with her right now if it's possible she does know."

I reminded myself that I was the medical proxy. The decision to keep Mother on life support or to remove her was mine. But I felt the need to enlist my sister's buy-in. I told the doctor I wanted to contact my sister to discuss the situation, and I let him know that she lived in France.

"How's her English?" he asked.

"Fine. But after decades there, she's probably better in French," I replied. Daniel nodded.

"Call her," said the doctor. "I'm fluent in French. I can explain to her the seriousness of your mother's condition."

I made the call. The doctor spoke, sometimes in English, sometimes in French. My sister answered, mostly in French. I watched Daniel, his mouth thin-lipped, fighting not to cry. He looked at me and tried to smile. Finally, my sister came back to me speaking English. "What do you think we should do?"

"I don't want to disconnect her. But in her living will she stated explicitly that she doesn't want to linger on life support. And I don't want her to suffer."

"Okay. If that's what Mommy wants, you can make that decision for her." I was relieved that my sister hadn't fought me to leave her on life support.

I nodded. "I'll give the consent to take her off life support," I said. "We'll all stay with her." We hung up and my sister began making plans to fly over to join us.

I gave the instruction to the nurses to disconnect Mother from the machines, to turn off her life. I have never had to do anything as painful as giving that consent. The nurses went in and disconnected her from the essential tubes and wires while we waited in the hall. When they were done, we rejoined Mother. Debbie stood beside me, held my right hand with her left and rested her other hand on my shoulder as I sat by the bed. Daniel and Anne stood at the foot of the bed with her. I held my mother's hand as she lay in the bed breathing her last breaths. She had most likely held me in a similar bed while I was breathing my first breaths. The room was quiet. A monitor beeped, and her pulse showed, a green line tracing across a black screen. I closed my eyes, unable to watch.

After several minutes Debbie leaned down and whispered, "She's gone. It's over now."

I sat for a couple of moments longer holding Mother's hand. Then I rushed from the room, bumping a nurse in the hall, crashing through the swinging doors back to the ICU lobby, finding my way back to the little living room where we had spoken with the doctor minutes earlier. Living room, I thought. Why do they call it a living room when it's where we come when people are dying?

Debbie came and sat with me. It was over. I cried briefly but was oddly empty. I had so much emotion when it came to my mother.

In the next weeks, we cleared out Mother's house, sold it, and closed her trust. She was gone.

Two regrets lingered. One goal I had always held was for her to recognize and approve of at least one of my accomplishments. Many times I was a disappointment to her by choosing to follow my own aspirations rather than hers. I had attained most of my personal goals but the successes I enjoyed were disappointments to her. I was satisfied, but her goals for me were not mine, and in her eyes I had failed by not pursuing her dreams. There was finality in the realization that I no longer had any chance of pleasing her. I hoped that wherever Mother was, she was looking back at me and was in fact proud of the things I had done, even if she never told me so.

And now there was also the recent discovery that the tales she shared about our family heritage might not be true. There were persistent questions about my family history. I know that Mother perpetuated her father James' convictions about our Scottish lineage, about her grandfather Oscar's service and imprisonment in Virginia during the Civil War, and other family stories. I had discovered that most of what she told me was not accurate. Maybe the stories were the ones her father had told her, and she honestly believed them. Maybe she was aware they weren't true but chose to accept and continue her father's revisions of our family's history. It could be that she created some of the tales herself to expand on her father's legacy. She would retreat whenever I asked about these inconsistencies. Her defensiveness as I asked questions about our heritage was either an effort to preserve her love for her father and his stories or an attempt to protect what she knew to be a lie.

Shortly before she died, it had gotten to the point that I couldn't discuss our family history with her. Now that she was gone, I might never know if what she related was fact or fiction. It was too late to get answers from Mother. I was on my own. Now I had to seek the truth with no more of her clues or deceptions.

My Quest Begins

LATE IN HER EIGHTIES, my mother began to sort through her things. "It will make it easier for you to clean out the house when I'm gone," she explained with sadness in her voice. She was old and wanted to rid herself of all the clutter she had accumulated, a sort of an end-of-life nesting, perhaps. On one visit to her house she led me to a basement closet, filled top to bottom and front to back with old books. Most of the books were decades-old paperbacks of little interest to me. We pulled them out one by one and sorted them. A few went into a black trash bag. The rest we stacked on the floor beside the closet. Mom believed they were worth keeping. We put all of them back in the closet when we finished culling out the throw-away books.

Near the bottom of the closet, buried among the paperbacks, were two antique books in a tattered paper grocery bag. Their spines were cracked, old leather covers faded and split. Their bindings were rotten, and the pages were worn and speckled. I have always loved old things, and I asked to keep the books and restore them. My mother replied, "Why bother? They were Oscar's. They're old. They're falling apart. Just throw them away." I kept them anyway and set about searching for book-binding companies.

The more notable of the two books was a big coffee table book bound with red leather and decorated with gold leaf. The spine was falling off, pages were loose, and the cover itself was frayed. It was titled *The Doré Gift*

Book: Illustrations to Tennyson's Idylls of the King. I researched the book and discovered that it was printed in London around 1872. If it was Oscar and Maggie's, as my mother suggested, it would have been a costly possession. Along with Tennyson's epic poem, thirty-seven engravings by the noted artist Gustav Doré were scattered throughout the book. They illustrated the Arthurian legend. Each engraving could stand alone as a masterful work of art. Collected together in the book, they were magnificent. I could wait to rebind the second book. The Doré book deserved to be first.

I found a bindery outside of Boston in the suburb of Woburn. I lived in Rhode Island, outside of Providence, and Woburn was more than an hour away, but one day when my work took me to Boston, I made a point of taking the Doré book with me and stopping by the bindery. It was in a small, weathered concrete factory building on a side street. The owner, a slight man with thinning hair and glasses, met me in the wood-floored lobby. Though there was an opened door to an office next to us, he led me around the corner, through the book binding factory and in a different door to the same office. It was evident he was a man of habits; this was how he always went to his office.

He summoned an elderly woman and told me she had been his favored worker with old books for years. Together they examined the Doré book, turning the pages carefully, holding them gingerly by the edges. They spoke admiringly of the artwork as I stood by. "We had Doré's book of *Dante's Paradise Lost* several years ago," the woman said. "But this is better. It's a more beautiful book, though a terribly tragic story."

"Can you fix the book?" I asked. I appreciated the Arthurian legends, but it was the book that interested me.

The owner replied, "Yes, we can redo the spine and bind the pages. I'll try to save the cover. It's too beautiful with the gold leaf for us to discard. It'll take at least a few weeks, maybe a month."

"How much will it cost?" I asked, holding my breath. I was hoping for less than two hundred dollars.

"Oh, I don't know," the owner said, his eyes averted. "This is delicate work. And it will be time consuming to do it right. It should be done absolutely perfectly. I won't allow anything less. But I don't want to set the price too high and have you decide not to preserve the book. The book is priceless."

I waited. The bindery owner fidgeted. The woman kept admiring the engravings, gently turning the pages. At last the owner whispered anxiously, "Could you afford seventy-five dollars? We'll try to keep it under one hundred."

"Sure. That's fine. When will it be ready?"

"Like I said, it will take a long time, probably a month. We'll call when it's ready."

He called two weeks later, and I went back to Boston. Again, the man led me around, through the factory to his office. We stood by the door to the lobby, and he showed me the Doré book. It was perfect! I asked how much I owed him. He answered apologetically, "Seventy-two dollars. I hope that's not too much."

"No, that's fine. How do you want it? Cash, check, or credit card?"

He shifted uncomfortably from foot to foot, tugging at the buttoned cuffs of his shirt sleeves. "Oh, I don't know. I don't like the business part of my business. However you want to pay me is fine."

I paid cash.

At first, the other book didn't seem like much. It was also old, with a gilt-lettered, brown leather cover pulling away from the bound pages. It was titled *The Flowers Personified*. Thumbing through it, I found engravings tinted with watercolors, probably by hand. They lacked the fine detail of Doré's work. The pictures were of flowers dressed as delicate maidens in gowns. A cursory scan of the text showed that it was unbearably romantic; poems and essays about the personalities and moods of different flowers. Originally written in French, it had been translated for this edition into English.

I was stunned to find an inscription carefully penned in flowing script on the first page:

Miss Maggie J. Teachout
From her Friend
Oscar E. McMurray
Christmas, 1865

My great-grandfather Oscar had given the book as a Christmas gift to his friend Maggie, the woman who would become his wife. This was right after the end of the Civil War.

With the Doré book restored, I took the Flowers book to a different bindery I had discovered near where I worked. It was in an old, abandoned mill north of Providence across the town line in Pawtucket. The building had been converted to contain a variety of eclectic small businesses: art studios, dance schools, and bars. Broken glass littered the parking lot. I went through a thick door, up a wide staircase to the third floor and down a long, dark echoing hallway lined with glass-paned doors. Small hand-lettered signs marked the businesses inside. The bindery was several doors down the hallway. It was run by a bearded, middle-aged Rhode Island School of Design graduate who had fallen in love with old books. He gathered his staff, several younger RISD grads, to examine my book. They were tattooed, pierced, dressed in black and shared their boss's affection for old books. They began examining *The Flowers Personified* with an eye to how they might restore it.

As they turned the pages, pressed flowers fell out. I picked them up and with their help compiled a list of what flowers had been set between which pages. The book binders appreciated that when it was rebound I would re-insert the flowers where they had been left by the previous owners of the book. They helped me store the flowers, a red maple leaf, a four-leaf clover, and other items in Ziploc bags. We also found needlepoint book marks, including one that read *Remember Me.* Who was it, I wondered, I was supposed to remember?

Inserted at page 303 was a memorial program recounting an "Address of the President of the Woman's Home Missionary Society of the Methodist Episcopal Church, Mrs. Rutherford B. Hayes at the Seventh Annual Meeting, Boston, Mass., November 1, 1888." The program indicated that Mrs. Hayes had died June 25, 1889 after delivering her address the previous November.

At the back of the book was a yellowed piece of folded paper covered with penciled notations of bible verses.

Clearly the book was special to Maggie. She had kept the book, cherished it, put flowers in it to press and stored other important mementos there. How many years had my great-grandparents Oscar and Maggie used the book as a place to preserve these special things? Oscar gave her the book a year and a half before their wedding in April, 1867, a date I found later in the family bible, another book my mother gave me. Online research informed me they lived near Albany, New York, at least when they were first married, but Maggie was in Boston twenty-two years later in 1889 for the Home Missionary Society meeting. Why? And my mother always told me that the MacMurray family had lived in New Jersey. Were they really from Albany?

I needed to know more about this couple, so I began to ask my mother questions. Her answers were vague, sometimes contradictory. Often she changed the subject, dismissive of my questions. She told me on several occasions, "I don't understand people who have an interest in their ancestry and try to trace their family tree. What if you discover a horse thief in your lineage?" I replied that it might be fun to know about a heritage that included horse thieves. And what if there were princes, kings, or other famous people in my past?

I probed for more information from my mother. The internet gave other clues. Slowly the story began to emerge. I became intrigued by Oscar and Maggie. Their blood is my blood. My DNA carries theirs forward. I want to know more about who I am, where I come from, what makes me, me.

3

They Meet:
Early Spring 1861

OSCAR SET THE LAST of the boxes into the cart, checked the harness, and led the horse out of the stable onto the dirt road toward Waterford. It was spring; the final traces of melting snow and rain had left the road damp. The horse clopped along, head down, hoof beats muffled by the mud. As he walked, leading the horse, Oscar thought about the news of a war far away with the rebellious southern states. Uncle Sylvester had enlisted at the start and had not been heard from since. Oscar worried what the war might mean for the brush business that employed him. Would sales lag if the war dragged on? Brushmaking was his livelihood. Mostly though, Oscar daydreamed about the girl.

It was a mile from his home in Lansingburgh to the bridge crossing the Hudson River to Waterford. It was a mile further to the warehouse on the bank of the canal where Oscar would sell the load of brushes entrusted to him for transport by his employer. Each Saturday, Oscar gathered boxes of brushes produced in the small Van Kleeck factory in Lansingburgh and in the smaller workshops behind the homes of brushmakers, from his relatives, the McMurray's, and from the other brushmakers who worked nearby. On Monday mornings at dawn he took his cargo up the road to Waterford.

For the past month, as he led his horse through Waterford, he had seen the girl walking along the street with a basket looped over her arm. When she heard his horse coming, she always stepped off the road to wait for him to pass, pulling her hoop skirt back so as not to be splashed by dirt from the horse or the cart. Each morning Oscar tipped his cap and smiled. "Good morning, Miss." And each time the girl smiled and replied, "Good morning to you as well."

That was all that had happened. But Oscar found himself thinking about the girl, looking forward to his weekly visits to Waterford, hoping to see her again, and hoping to find a way to meet her.

Today was Monday, and he was on his way. He crossed the bridge, looking along the junctions of the new canal system that connected Waterford to Albany, the Hudson River and New York City to the south and running along the Mohawk River, through the Erie Canal locks all the way to Buffalo far to the west. The canals were the engine that drove the economy of the region.

On the street in Waterford, Oscar began watching for the girl. He usually began his trip at dawn, but he had started earlier each week, seeing the girl sooner and sooner along the street. Today he dawdled, hoping to discover where she lived.

There she was, running down the steps from the wide porch of a three-story house, opening the low gate to the street, watching for him. She stopped outside the gate and waited for Oscar and his horse and cart to pass. Oscar saw a second woman come out on the porch of the house and heard her call to the girl, her voice stern. "What are you waiting for Jennie? Hurry along now. You have your errands at the market, and there's school and some work for you here at the house when you get back. Run along."

The girl answered, "Yes, Mother." She turned and began walking briskly, the basket over her arm, her head down. Once she was hidden from the house by trees, she slowed her pace and stopped.

Oscar looked to the house and tipped his cap to the dark-haired woman standing there. "Good morning, Ma'am."

"Morning," she replied. Then she was back inside the house closing the glass-paneled oak door behind her.

"Jennie! Her name is Jennie!" he thought, exulting at the knowledge.

The girl waited. Oscar came to her and stopped as well, holding the horse's harness as though he was checking it. "Good morning, Miss."

The girl smiled, her face lighting up. "Good morning to you!"

"I heard your mother call to you. Your name is Jennie?"

"Yes. No. It's Margaret Jane Teachout. Somehow when I was little my parents started calling me by my middle name and it became Jennie. My friends call me Maggie."

"Well, then, Maggie. I'm Oscar McMurray. From Lansingburgh."

"And what do you do here in Waterford every Monday with your horse and cart?"

"I'm a brushmaker. We're all brushmakers in my family. My boss has given me the task of bringing the brushes to Waterford each week to sell. It's a lot of responsibility for a seventeen year old man."

"Seventeen? I just turned thirteen last week."

Oscar looked at her carefully. It was the first time they had been this close to each other. Yes, she was young. That wasn't a concern for him. She was very pretty. Her dark hair was parted in the middle, twisted into a thick braid behind her head. Her eyes were wide-set and filled with laughter. She was small, barely as tall as Oscar's shoulder though Oscar was not a big man. Her dress was dark, thin linen for the early springtime warmth. She wore a black woven cord necklace.

Maggie looked back at Oscar and giggled. He was the most handsome man she had ever seen. She blushed slightly. "It is a pleasure to meet you, Oscar McMurray."

"The pleasure is mine, Maggie Teachout. Could I meet you again? Before next Monday morning?" It was a bold question, but he needed to know.

"I should like that. You know where I live. Could you come calling on the weekend?"

"I will come to visit on Saturday afternoon." He nodded and tipped his cap. Maggie grinned again, excited by the Saturday arrangement.

Reluctantly Oscar turned back to the horse. "I must be going now. I have a load of brushes to sell. Good day to you."

"I will tell my parents to expect you Saturday afternoon."

They had accomplished what they both hoped to do on that Monday morning. There was nothing left for them to say. Oscar shook the horse's lead and began walking with the wagon. Maggie walked next to him heading to market. Both smiled, looking at the road ahead of them, sneaking looks across at each other. At the corner Oscar turned his horse and cart toward the distributor's warehouse on the bank of the canal. Maggie kept on straight.

"Good day, Maggie Teachout. Till Saturday."

"Good day, Oscar McMurray."

*****

Oscar spent Saturday morning gathering boxes of brushes from his family, stopping in each of the tiny shops they all had behind their houses. He went to neighbors' houses and collected their newly made brushes as well. He stacked all the brush boxes inside the cramped workshop he shared with his father, ready to load the cart with the factory-made brushes on Monday morning. Stiff cardboard square-cornered boxes, each labeled on the lid "E. Van Kleeck Brushmaking – Lansingburgh, New York" filled half his shop.

His work for the week completed, Oscar bathed, shaved, and put on his dark Sunday suit, a stiffly starched white shirt, and a wide black silk tie. His parents noticed of course.

"Well, Oscar, what is this? Today is Saturday. You're preparing for church a day early?"

"There is a young lady in Waterford. I plan to call on her this afternoon."

His mother looked satisfied. "Who is this young lady? What is her name?"

"Maggie Teachout. I'll be meeting her family today, I expect."

His father smiled and chuckled. "Be a gentleman, son. Take a gift for her and her family. Perhaps some flowers?"

"I plan to. I've set aside a brush I made to give to her."

"Be home for supper," advised his mother. "Don't overstay your welcome. This is your first visit with the young lady and her family."

Oscar walked the route he took each Monday, eager for his visit with Maggie. The road dragged on forever. He paused on the bridge to Waterford and wiped the dust off his freshly polished shoes with the cuffs of his black trousers. Then he leaned down to knock the dust off his cuffs with his hands. He wiped his hands on a white linen handkerchief and smoothed his dark curls into place. Ready, he walked the few blocks through Waterford to Maggie's house. In through the gate, up the short walk, up the steps, across the wide porch, and Oscar was at her door. He knocked on the frosted glass pane, his heart pounding.

A tall man, chin-bearded, opened the door. "Yes?"

"I'm Oscar McMurray. From Lansingburgh. I've come to call on Margaret. Is she home today?"

"Yes, she is. We've been expecting you. I'm her father. Why don't you wait here on the porch? I'll go find Maggie and her mother."

Oscar stood anxiously, sweating. In a few moments Maggie's father returned with his wife and with Maggie. The girl's mother carried a tray, set with four tall glasses and a plate. The father led them to four white wicker chairs set in a circle around a low table on the porch. "We will sit here," he announced. Oscar stood while Maggie sat. Her father sat next to her. Oscar settled into a chair across from Maggie leaving the chair on Maggie's right for her mother.

Mother put down the tray and set out the four glasses of pale lemonade in front of each chair. Then she offered Oscar a stack of cloth napkins and a small plate with four cookies on it. "Would you care for lemonade and a cookie?"

"Thank you very much." Oscar took the cookie and a napkin self-consciously, making sure every word, every gesture was delivered with perfect etiquette. His eyes kept straying across to Maggie. Each time he looked she caught his eyes and smiled.

Mother offered a cookie to Maggie next, then to her husband. Finally, she sat with the last cookie and napkin and her glass of lemonade.

Father spoke first. "Margaret tells us that you are a brushmaker."

"Yes sir. It's my family's business. We all work for Van Kleeck's Brushmakers down in Lansingburgh. Here, let me show you. I've brought a small brush I made."

Oscar took the brush from his pocket. It was delicate, narrow, and barely as long as the palm of his hand. The handle was dark maple, inlaid with white ash, curved, beveled, and polished smooth as a river stone. The horse-hair bristles were as soft as rabbit fur and patterned with whorls of red, green, yellow, and white. He had painted a pattern of flowers on the back of the handle. It was a beautiful work of art, not a utilitarian brush. Oscar handed it to Maggie's father.

He inspected the brush, turning it over and over, feeling the soft bristles, rubbing his thumb over the smooth wood. "Very nice. Very pretty. You earn your living selling brushes like this?" He handed the brush across to Mother.

"No sir. Most of the brushes I make are hardier. Boot brushes, clothes brushes, hat brushes. Brushes for hair or for shaving. Scrub brushes and brushes for horses. All types of brushes. They sell very nicely. I make an adequate wage. I made this little brush just to be beautiful. It's not for sale. It's a gift."

"Very good. Thank you very much. Mother, why don't you give it to Jennie? I believe the young man intended it for her?" He looked to Oscar for confirmation as he stated the last question. Oscar nodded.

Mother handed the brush to Maggie. Maggie grinned, her mouth open in wonder as she examined the brush, sliding the soft bristles across her palm. "Thank you, Oscar. It's lovely."

Oscar stayed for only an hour. When the lemonade was gone, he stood. "Thank you very much for the lemonade but I must be leaving. My family is expecting me to return for supper."

Maggie and her parents stood. Her father shook Oscar's hand and said, "If you would like to visit Jennie... Maggie again next week you would be welcomed. She is a young girl but you are a good man."

"I would very much like to visit again."

Oscar shook Mother's hand and finally Maggie's. Her palm was warm in his grasp. Then he turned to the steps. "Good day," he said.

He was down the steps, along the walk to the gate. He stopped there and turned to look back. Maggie was between her parents on the porch hugging her mother. All were smiling. Oscar gave a quick wave and repeated, "Good day." Maggie grinned and waved back. Then he was gone, taking the road back to his home in Lansingburgh, laughing quietly once or twice as he walked. He was whistling by the time he got home.

4

Bible Stories

AT FIRST, I WAS puzzled. I noticed that in *The Flowers Personified* Oscar had signed his last name McMurray. My mother had always stressed that we were MacMurray's, Mac with an "a." We are Scottish, she insisted, with a long though undefined Scottish family tradition. She obsessed that only members of the Murray clan were entitled to wear the Murray and royal Stuart tartans, as though there were "Tartan Police" lurking, ready to hold unworthy people accountable for wearing the wrong tartans. McMurray might be Irish. Given my mother's reluctance to discuss our heritage, I knew better than to confront this question directly with her.

On a visit to her house, I showed her the two rebound books. "Oh, they're lovely," she said. "I'm so glad I saved them for you." I recalled her fretting that they were old and broken and should be thrown away.

"Mom, you gave me those two old books. And yes, I had them rebound, and they turned out nicely. Do we possibly have a family bible?"

"Of course. Let me show you." She led me to some bookshelves set into the wall in a hallway. The cluttered shelves held a hodge-podge of old things; bookends that might have been busts of Dante and Beatrice, more old books, a grimy plastic globe that showed central Africa as "The Belgian Congo." Newspaper clippings from her square dance club and papers from a Girl Scout troop she had sponsored decades earlier were tucked in among the books.

"There," Mother said, pointing. "The Bible's on the top shelf. See if you can take it down." She was tiny and couldn't reach it.

The bible was heavy, possibly weighing twenty pounds. I managed to drag it down without knocking other objects off the lower shelves. It was an impressive tome, more than a foot tall, eleven inches wide, and four inches thick. The cover was dark brown leather stretched front and back over sculpted wood and embossed with gold leaf. The pages were edged with gold. Holding it closed were two wide metal clasps, dark with a patina.

I thumbed through it quickly hoping to find family records. Traditionally families have listed important life events in their family bibles. The book was cumbersome and included biblical history and maps as well as the scriptures. Although there were many pages and sections in addition to the scriptures, I couldn't find any family records on my first cursory inspection. When I explained to my mother what I was looking for, she became impatient. "Let's get some iced tea and cookies," she fussed. "Just put the bible back up on the shelf. This is a waste of time."

"Could I bring it home and keep it with the other books? I showed you how well they turned out. I would preserve this bible, and I could take my time looking for family records."

"No. This book is in fine condition. It doesn't need any of that work. Besides, I read it all the time. I need to keep it here."

She made me return it to the high shelf where we had found it, because it was too heavy for her to lift. I knew enough not to question how she could read it all the time if she kept it too high for her to reach.

Months later, when, in a forgetful moment, she allowed me to take the bible home with me, I discovered her true motive in keeping it from me. Marriages, births, and deaths were listed in a section in the middle, beginning with James Teachout, Maggie's father. Then Oscar and Maggie are listed, and there are listings of many MacMurrays and Teachouts over the decades until the marriage of my grandmother Grace Cooper to my grandfather James H. MacMurray, one of Oscar and Maggie's children. My mother's birth is one of the last listings: Elma MacMurray, born April 7, 1921. All of the names and dates are carefully penned with the same handwriting.

These are the key entries. Margaret J. Teachout was born May 25, 1848, the second of four children in Waterford, New York. There was no date given for Oscar's birth, but later research indicated he was born August 27, 1843.

Oscar E. MacMurray and Margaret J. Teachout are recorded in the bible as being married on April 4, 1867 in Waterford. Oscar was going on twenty-four. Maggie was a month shy of nineteen. They had four children, Carrie, born in May 13, 1868, Eugene, born May 8, 1872, James H. MacMurray, my grandfather, born on August 29, 1875, and Edna, born June 6, 1891.

Edna was the first to pass away, on July 29, 1892, little more than a year old. None of Oscar and Maggie's other children have dates listed for their deaths. Oscar died July 2, 1907, when he was almost sixty-four years old. Maggie lived until December 11, 1921. She was seventy-three.

James H. MacMurray married my grandmother, Grace Cooper in Maplewood, New Jersey on May 29, 1920. James was forty-four years old. My mother was their only child, born April 7, 1921, almost a year after the wedding. Grandmother Maggie passed away eight months later.

I learned several things by reviewing the family records. I was not aware that my grandfather James had three siblings. I had heard of Carrie and a bit about Gene. But I had never heard of poor Edna who only lived a year. I knew that James, my mother's father, had died while she was in college, and I assumed he must have died young. He had married later in life and was in his mid-sixties. My grandmother Grace was the only one of these ancestors that I'd met.

And, every time the name was listed, it was spelled MacMurray with an "a," not McMurray. So why had Oscar written it McMurray in *The Flowers Personified*? I asked my mother.

"Oh. He must have misspelled it when he wrote it in the book," she said.

I wasn't buying it. No one misspells their own name. I needed to dig deeper. MacMurray or McMurray, who were these people? How did they make their living? What were they like? Where were they from?

My mother continued to discourage my search for my roots. But she fed my interest in old things from our family. I discovered more and more treasures at my mother's house. One was a detailed pencil drawing of a sailing ship on a piece of heavy-stock yellowed paper. The picture showed a nice artistic talent. The ship has billowing sails, shaded and trimmed with lines. An American flag flaps in the rigging at the stern. Men are on the deck. Carefully drawn rows of waves are alongside the ship. At the bottom of the drawing is the title: "U.S. Brig of War – Avenger." Carefully penciled in the waves at the bow of the ship is the artist's signature. "Oscar E. MacMurray – 1857." Given the date of birth I discovered for him, he was only fourteen years old at the time he created this fine drawing. It hinted at the detailed craftsmanship he would later employ with his brushmaking, his profession, as a grown man.

"Perhaps you get your artistic talent from your great-grandfather Oscar," my mother said.

My mother had often mentioned that Oscar was a brushmaker. We had several antique brushes lying around the house. Mother gave me a few. One, a shoe brush, is shaped like a fanciful animal of some sort. It has two brushes built into it. One, the "head" of the animal, is a small brush to apply shoe polish. The other, a brush along the long belly of the animal, would be used to buff the shoes to a shine. The bristles are black and white, set in clusters so that they alternate stripes like a zebra. The handle is two wood tones, layered and inlaid with graceful curves. A long, curving piece of the handle is the animal's tail. Making brushes like this was how Oscar earned his living. Two other brushes are smaller, impractical, but very pretty, showing Oscar's artistry. One has an inlaid polished wooden handle painted with tiny flowers.

I also found a man's straight razor among mom's old things. The handle is carved ivory showing a nude woman surrounded by flowers. Could the razor be Oscar's? Would he have owned such a thing? It's a beautiful piece of art that a man would have enjoyed. But is this to his taste, or would it have been inappropriate for a man of his moral compass? I don't know. What kind of a man was Oscar? Each item I discovered traces back to some long-departed relative, but who? Each raises more questions.

Who were these people?

Mother also gave me four very old daguerreotypes set into hinged, carved black wood cases. Inside, the pictures were framed with gold filigree. One had two pictures; a solemn bearded man on the left side and a black-robed woman on the right. Mother told me they were of Oscar and Maggie. Later, matching against other old photographs, I suspect they were Maggie's parents.

I was more certain about the other three daguerreotypes. Two had only a woman's picture on the right side, again framed with gold. The left side was lined with pressed red velvet. Stuck onto the velvet on each of them was a small green paper labeling them as "Mother MacMurray." The woman in both was a tiny, pretty girl with curly dark hair parted in the middle and pulled behind her head. She was almost smiling, a mischievous Mona Lisa look. There was also a black wood case with a picture of a man. He had thick wavy dark hair and a trimmed mustache. In the early 1970s, when I too had long hair and a mustache, my mother had shown this daguerreotype to me and commented, "You look just like your great-grandfather Oscar."

There they were. I now had pictures of Oscar and Maggie, but I still knew so little about them.

Oscar Enlists:
1861-1862

IT HAD BEEN SIX months since the start of the war with the fall of Fort Sumter in South Carolina. In May, 1861, only weeks after that news came to Lansingburgh and Waterford, the 2nd New York Volunteer regiment mustered at Washington Square in Troy, ready to be deployed. Oscar stood with Maggie in the crowd, anxiously watching the eager ranks of new soldiers. He was sweating as much from nerves as the heat. He wiped his face with his white linen handkerchief and then reached to hold Maggie's hand. He was silent.

Maggie beamed with the excitement. A military band was playing lively marches, and the new recruits stood proudly with their families, their wives and girlfriends, showing off their bright new blue uniforms. Sunlight gleamed from the brass, the cornets and tubas, the uniform buttons, the braid on the officers' epaulets. It was a festive moment, and Maggie felt like cheering until she saw Oscar's pale face.

She pulled him to the side of the park, away from the gaiety, and sat with him on a bench in the cool shade of an elm tree. "Oscar, what's the matter?"

"It scares me. I think about my uncle Sylvester. He's one of my best friends, like my big brother. We call him Stub because he's short, but he's got a strong, thick body, and he's always been a fighter. Stub enlisted with the

123rd New York Volunteers as soon as the war started. He couldn't wait to go. He thought it would be a great adventure, a chance for him to do something special, to make a difference in the world. We haven't heard from him since he left. I worry every day that he's been killed somewhere down south. And I see these men here, all excited to go fight the rebels. Stub was like that before he left, and I think of how many of these boys will march down the road in a few minutes and never come back."

"Oh Oscar. Oh, my dear. They'll come back. What they're doing is for such a noble, heroic cause. They're freeing the slaves from that ungodly abomination of slavery. Of course they'll come home. So will Stub. Do you think you should enlist?"

"I don't know. I'm only seventeen, but that's almost old enough. I could find a way to go if I really wanted to. But I don't."

"Why not? It would be such a good thing for you to do. Just like your uncle Stub."

"There are so many reasons I don't want to go. I wonder sometimes if maybe the southern states have a right to do what they're doing. I mean, I agree that slavery is awful. They shouldn't have it in the rebellious states. I disagree with their way of life, but I think they might have the right to secede. There are so many things to consider. And I also see President Lincoln's need to preserve the Union of all the states. We are a better country if we are united. We need to bring the rebellious states back. But would I kill to preserve the Union? I'm not sure. I know I don't want to die for that cause."

"You'll be fine." Maggie reached for his hand, considering his words, balancing them against her own ideals. She understood what he was saying, but she was so passionate about abolition. Slavery was awful, and it had to end.

She continued, "Have you read any of the things written by Frederick Douglass? It's such a terrible thing, slavery. Even if they have the right to secede, they ought to get rid of slavery. You must believe abolition is a worthwhile cause to fight for?"

"Of course. Yes, I know it is." Oscar nodded, loving Maggie but frustrated by her innocent view of things. None of the people in Lansingburgh seemed to understand. They all seemed to think war was some glamorous lark, like a day going camping with no risks, no danger. But Oscar didn't believe it was like that. He'd studied his history in school and he knew. This was a war, and people got killed in wars.

He tried to support Maggie. "I like how passionate you are about abolition. So many other girls I know don't care about things like that. They don't understand political things at all."

"Well, I do. I read a lot about many things. Someday women will be able to vote, and I'll be ready. Women here and in England are already preparing for that day."

Oscar nodded. "I worry about what the war will do to the economy if it lasts. Not just here in Lansingburgh and in Troy and Albany and Waterford but all over the country. Our brush business is already showing the strain after just a few months. And what would Mr. Van Kleeck do if I and many of the others left? How would he run his business without us? This is bad. If the war lasts a long time it could really hurt businesses all over the country."

"But it won't last. Don't you see? We are fighting for a just cause. God will be on our side. And we have so many more men to send than the rebellious states do. We will win. It will be over quickly." Maggie was confident in her assertion.

Oscar shook his head. "You read a lot. Do you read the newspapers? We don't get much information about the war. We're way up here on the Hudson River. But what I read is that the war is not going very well. The Union has lost many of the battles. Men are getting killed in the south. Lots of them. It's a terrible thing. Those men getting ready to leave for the war, over there in the park? They've signed on for two years."

"It won't last that long. The more men we send, the sooner it will be over. You should enlist."

"Maggie, look at me. I'm an artisan, an artist. I make brushes for a living. I don't turn eighteen till late in August. I've never fired a rifle or even been in a fist fight. I'm afraid I wouldn't make a very good soldier."

"You would be a marvelous soldier. You'd come home to me a hero."

"I'm not a hero to you right now?"

Maggie looked down shyly. She and Oscar had been courting for less than two months. She took Oscar's hand again, checking that no one in the park could see them sitting like this together. "Of course you're my hero. I love you."

Oscar gave her hand a brief squeeze. She squeezed back quickly. He thought about how young she was, how naïve she was about the real things that happened in the world. And he loved her.

"All right," he said. "Let's do this. If a year from now the war is still going on, then I'll enlist. If it's over sooner, I won't have to. Would that be all right? I'll be a year older by then and better prepared to go. And if the war is still going on a year from now, I expect they'll need even a poor soldier like me."

The band was playing again, a lively marching tune, setting the ranks of recruits in motion down the dirt road to the dock. Oscar stood, ready to go watch the parade. Maggie stood as well but pulled him to her and gave his cheek a hurried brush of her lips. "You'll make a fine soldier someday," she whispered.

They stood together and watched the four hundred men in the 2nd New York Volunteer regiment marching down to the river, ready to board the barges heading south to New York City and on to the war. The men grinned and waved to their cheering families, their wives, and their sweethearts. It was a jubilant time for the little city of Troy.

For a moment Oscar wanted to make Maggie proud of him the way these families were proud of their departing men. But he knew deep in his heart that he was not a soldier.

*****

It was late October 1862, and more than a year had passed. Oscar sat next to Maggie on the overstuffed red sofa in her parlor. Two china teacups with the shallow remains of cooling tea sat on the table next to them. Her parents were in the kitchen, discreetly chaperoning from a distance, giving the couple some privacy to talk. "I've done it," Oscar said. "I enlisted this morning." His voice lacked enthusiasm.

"Oh Oscar! I'm so proud of you. I know you said last year that you would enlist when we watched that regiment march off to the war. I've been waiting for you to say this. You'll be fighting to free the slaves. It's such a wonderful thing you're doing."

Oscar nodded, unsmiling though he appreciated her support. "I'll start my training next week. And I'll be mustered in and then sent south a few weeks later. I've already told Mr. Van Kleeck. He understood, and he told me he'll put me back to work if I come home from the war."

"If you come home? Of course you'll come home. Why wouldn't you?"

"It's a war, Maggie. It's dangerous. The rebels will be trying to kill me. And I don't know the first thing about fighting. I'm a bit frightened. But I know this is the right thing to do."

"You'll be fine. I'll pray for you every day. They'll train you to be a soldier before you leave." She reached over and gave his hand a reassuring pat.

"I'm worried that when I go, I won't ever get home to see you again."

Maggie leaned forward, her hands folded in her lap and looked at him. For the first time she felt his fear. What if he was right? What if he got hurt while he was fighting? It came to her suddenly that her ideals mattered little when it came to rebel soldiers who would be trying to kill Oscar, her love. What if he never came home?

"How long will you be gone?" she asked.

"It's only for nine months. That's all the time they think they'll need us now. They believe the war will be over in less than a year."

"Good. You'll be training here?"

"Yes, for several weeks. After that I don't know where they'll send me. Or even exactly when I'll be leaving, but I need to see you every day before I go. Every moment is precious."

"Yes, and we'll write to each other every day while you're gone."

Four weeks later Oscar marched to the docks on the Hudson with the 177th Regiment of the New York National Guard.

Unlike the joyous departure of the 2nd Regiment in the spring a year earlier this deployment was somber. Bare trees and the damp chill of late upstate autumn added to the foreboding. A band played brightly, and the crowd that watched the departing soldiers tried to infuse the moment with enthusiasm. They cheered 400 more men being sent south to win the war. His mother and father and Maggie with her parents clapped and cheered. He waved and managed a smile for Maggie as he marched past. The two families stood on the riverbank as his boat moved out through the fog into the current and was swept down the Hudson to New York City.

Colonel Ainsworth had made a short speech to the crowd and told them that their men would be safe under his command. He seemed capable enough but even he had no idea where they would be deployed when they left New York for the war. Maggie couldn't allow herself to worry. Oscar would be fine. He had to be fine. God was watching over him.

Oscar had been trained in how to drill, how to march, and how to keep his rifle oiled and ready. He had not had any target practice. Ammunition was too valuable to waste on practice.

Oscar kept a small photograph of Maggie, printed from a silver plate, folded inside a pad of paper in the breast pocket of his uniform. He began tallying the days till he could return to her, marking them with a short pencil on the paper. He vowed to himself that he would mount Maggie's picture in a suitable frame if he survived. One way or another he would keep her and the photograph with him forever.

Maggie had a card with a picture of Oscar as well. Oscar had had the photograph taken several days before he mustered into the 177th. It showed him in his uniform, brass buttons down the front of the oversized blue coat, the sleeves cuffed with a single chevron stripe and more brass buttons. His cap rested near his elbow as he leaned on a column in the photographer's studio. He looked as noble and heroic as he could in the photograph, but a trace of his trepidation showed in his eyes. Still, he was the handsome man she loved. He had to stay safe while he was away from her. She hid the card in a drawer in a small table beside her bed. Every night before she went to sleep, she took out the card, kissed Oscar's picture and said a prayer for his safety.

The Scarlet Letter A

MY MOTHER HAD CALLED me to come for a visit to help her sort through some old photographs. When I arrived, she began pulling boxes full of pictures out from under the bed in a guest bedroom. Most were early Kodachrome, yellowed and faded. She found more pictures stuffed in envelopes in a desk drawer. We looked at Christmases and birthday celebrations from many years ago. Some of the people in the photos were no more than vague memories, even their names forgotten. We discarded most of the photos. A few hundred we deemed worthy of keeping. We put these back in their frayed envelopes and broken shoe boxes and slid them under the bed for safe-keeping.

While digging through the desk drawer, I came across a piece of stiff paper, faded beige and held in a crimped roll by a brittle red rubber band. The band broke when I took it off to unroll the paper. What was on the paper was striking; it was the wedding certificate for Oscar and Maggie. An ornamental flowered border circled the paper. At the top was an etching showing a young couple holding hands at the altar rail in the front of a church. The girl looked down demurely and clutched a small bouquet in her left hand. She held her new husband's hand with her right. A small crowd of family and friends gathered behind them. The minister stood at the rail, blessing the young newlyweds.

The faces of the couple didn't look like the old photographs I had seen of

Oscar and Maggie but how could I debate the words that had been filled in with black ink in a careful script on the stock form. The date matched the wedding day of Oscar and Maggie.

This is to Certify
That *Mr. O.E. McMurray* of *Lansingburgh* in the State of
N.Y. and *Miss Maggie Teachout* of *Waterford*
In the State of *N.Y.* were by me joined together in
HOLY MATRIMONY
On the *Fourth* day of *April* in the Year of our Lord
One Thousand Eight Hundred and *Sixty Seven*.
Jas. J. Eddy   *Hiram E. Serlon*
Lottie E. Sweeney   *Minister of M.E. Church, Waterford*

I assumed that Mr. Eddy and Miss Sweeney were friends of Oscar and Maggie who signed the certificate after witnessing the ceremony.

There it was again. McMurray without the letter "a." Not MacMurray. Some places I had found the name MacMurray, notably in the family Bible. Others, like "The Flowers Personified," showed it as McMurray. I recalled my mother explaining that Oscar must have misspelled his name when he signed the "Flowers" book for his friend Maggie. It made no sense.

What should I make of all this? MacMurray would make my family line Scottish. McMurray would be Irish. My online searches for Oscar had always pointed to a McMurray spelling. And the Oscar E. McMurray I had traced who was always connected with Maggie Teachout lived in Lansingburgh, New York. But my mother believed he was from New Jersey, where she was born. She told me she thought they may have come to New Jersey directly from Nova Scotia, "where many Scottish first came to North America." "Nova Scotia is Latin for New Scotland," she said. "It was a place that reminded many of the early settlers of their homeland."

Now proof was building, an overwhelming amount of evidence pointing to the name McMurray and an origin in Lansingburgh and Waterford, New York. I quietly re-rolled the marriage certificate and brought it with me to my home in Rhode Island, planning to preserve it in a frame.

At home, I checked in the family Bible. MacMurray. I evaluated the signature on the old drawing of the sailing ship. MacMurray again, but looking at the name closely I noticed that the letter "a" was originally a small letter "c." It has been modified, a pencil line added to change the "c" to the letter "a." A new letter "c" had been tucked in before the Murray. It became clear to me that history had been re-written changing my great-grandfather's name to make us a family of Scottish rather than Irish descent. Why? When? And by whom?

Several weeks later I visited my mother again. I had to get to the bottom of the mystery. "Mom, I've been looking into the lives of Oscar and Maggie. And I keep coming up against the name McMurray rather than MacMurray. I don't understand."

"Maybe it's a different Oscar McMurray. It's a common name. And his wife's name was Margaret, not Maggie."

"No mom, this is Oscar and Maggie from Lansingburgh, New York. They had a son named James H. MacMurray who lived in New Jersey, and that's your father. Oscar also had a son Eugene and a daughter Carrie. I've heard you mention Eugene once or twice, and you've talked a good bit about Aunt Carrie. This is your grandfather. But it's always McMurray rather than MacMurray. It doesn't make sense to me."

She gave a resigned sigh. "Well you see," she said, her voice taking on the sing-song tone of a teacher reciting a memorized lesson to a child. "They were Scottish. But there was a war in Scotland and England over the succession to the throne. Bonnie Prince Charlie, you know. There was the Battle of Cologne or some such place. And it became difficult for the supporters of the Bonnie Prince to stay in Scotland. So, our family may have gone to Ireland for a while to be safe. Then they would have come to Nova Scotia from there, but they were still Scottish, not Irish."

"How long were they in Ireland?"

"I don't know," she replied, exasperated. "A few years possibly. Maybe one or two generations. But they were still Scottish. They were never like those Irish. We are certainly not Irish!"

In my mind I could hear my mother scoffing at Irish day-laborers as she sometimes did, taking me to task for my appreciation of good beer. "The Irish lack the breeding and class we expect from people. I can still see them coming home from working at their menial jobs, sitting on their front stoops in their undershirts, sweating and drinking beer straight from the bottle." It all made sense to me now. My mother and possibly her father James had a thing about the Irish. They wanted to believe that they were better in some way. I should grow up to be better as well. I am Scottish after all. I shouldn't drink beer or sit on my front porch in a t-shirt.

"But Mom," I said, "People who come to the United States become American after a few years. People born here are Americans. One or two generations and they are American. Wouldn't it be that way for a Scottish family who moved to Ireland? After one or two generations wouldn't they be Irish rather than Scottish? And what about the Irish spelling of the last name?"

"They were Scottish," she insisted, becoming angry. "I don't know how long they might have lived in Ireland. They were still Scottish. Anyway, if they did live in Ireland it must have been Northern Ireland, the Protestant section. They *never* would have lived in the Catholic part of the country."

"Mom, when I checked your uncle Eugene on the internet, he always came up McMurray. But he's Oscar's son, just like your father. Oscar is always a McMurray, too, when I find him online. But your father is MacMurray. And in the family Bible and in other places the name is MacMurray. I'm still confused."

"Well, Eugene was a MacMurray too, but he changed his name to become a McMurray. He was an architect you see, and he got contracts to build Catholic churches, cathedrals in New Jersey. It was easier for him to get the business contracts if they thought he was Irish and a Catholic."

"Mom, both he and your father and Aunt Carrie seem to have been born McMurray. So Eugene didn't have to change his name. He was already a McMurray, just like his father Oscar and his mother Maggie."

"I don't know," she said, her frustration beginning to turn her tone again to anger. "My father was close with Aunt Carrie. He took care of her because she never married, you know. And they were both MacMurrays. Why Eugene's name is different I just don't know. He didn't really have much to do with our family, you see."

I knew enough to walk away from a brewing fight. So I let the matter drop. I didn't bring it up again though my mother came back to the name issue several times in the years ahead, always to stress that we were MacMurrays and ought to be proud of our refined Scottish heritage. We never spoke of the Irish. I continued to search for my heritage but without her knowledge.

When I mentioned my discovery to my children, my daughter Carey laughed. "Ha! So we're Irish. Nice!" Irish or Scottish, life went on as usual for her.

My son David was thrilled. His mother-in-law's maiden name is Hogan. The Hogan's are proudly southern and Irish. To his wife's family, David was still a Yankee from New England, but now at least with his Irish roots he fit in with the Hogan relatives. He celebrated on the next St. Patrick's Day, sharing the Hogan family's special recipe for homemade Irish Cream. Then again, he always had celebrated on St. Patrick's Day, but now he had an excuse. The next Christmas he and his wife Teri gave me a Christmas tree ornament. It was a grinning red-haired boy in an Aran Isle cable knit sweater holding a sign that read "Born Irish." My mother never noticed the ornament on our tree. And I never pointed it out to her.

7

Confederate Money

WHEN I WAS A little boy my family lived in Lynchburg, Virginia, where my father was a young physics professor at Randolph Macon Women's College. I recall my mother taking me aside one morning to show me a string-bound package. She opened it and handed me a stack of dollar bills.

"This is Confederate money," she explained. "Your great-grandfather fought in the Civil War, but he was captured and put in a prisoner of war camp not far from here. When the war ended he came home, and he must have brought this money with him."

I looked at the bills. I was young and didn't really understand money. To me a dollar was a dollar, and you bought things with dollars. "We're rich, mom! Look at how much money you have!"

"Oh, this is worthless," she said. "The rebels lost the war so now it's just paper. But I suspect that the local people know somehow that we have this money. That's why the people here in Virginia hate us. They must know that my grandfather Oscar was a prisoner of war near here and that he took their money home with him. I know they're always looking at me and thinking, 'there goes that damn Yankee lady.' Some of what they think of me is because of the traditional town and gown problem. People who lack a good education always envy those of us who are well-read, who have culture and breeding. We live in a town of poorly educated people. That's why we spend most of our time with the faculty here. We're accepted in academia. The local people don't like the professors. And they also hate me because I'm a Yankee."

She put the money away, and I didn't see it again for years. I sat back as a boy, confused by this early lesson in human relations. I had no idea that the town disliked us. I never felt it. And why would they? Because my father worked at a college? Because my mother was from New Jersey? It made no sense, but I stored away her lesson. A few years later we moved to Boston when my father took a new position at Boston University.

Several more times I heard my mother commenting on Virginians' dislike for her because of her Yankee roots. Decades later my wife Debbie and I retired and moved back to Williamsburg, Virginia, because both of my children had gone to college in Virginia and settled there. A few months after I moved to Williamsburg, I brought my mother to visit, wanting to show her my new house and the wonderful town where I now lived. Near the end of her visit she said it again. "How can you live here? Your neighbors are all looking at me and thinking there goes that damn Yankee woman."

"What? Mom, you haven't even met my neighbors, let alone spoken with them. Why do you think that?"

"I can tell. I see the way they watch us when you drive out of the neighborhood. Southerners are like that."

"Mom, most of my neighbors aren't from the south, or even Virginia. My neighbor on one side is from Pakistan, I think. He doesn't really interact with anyone in the neighborhood. And on the other side there's a Korean family. Across the street there's a husband and wife from Pennsylvania. And there's a Polish immigrant across the street too, and a mixed-race family from Winnipeg two doors down. It's a very diverse neighborhood. They come from all over. Why would you think they don't like you because you're from the north? They don't know you, and they don't really care where you come from."

"They know. Oh yes! And maybe it's because we're well educated and they're not. They know."

"Mom, the town is very well educated. The College of William and Mary is only a few miles away, and people here respect education."

"It's the south. No, they don't."

She was my mom. I took her as she was. There was no point arguing with her about whether my neighbors hated her.

A year later, after she died, I began sorting through the piles of old documents and boxes of forgotten treasures we found stored in her house. I found a fat manila envelope filled with papers relating to her family and their past. Among the papers was the packet of confederate money. It was folded into a sheet of gold foil paper. The foil paper had writing on the back in a careful ink script. "Confederate Officers used to trim their hat during the war in 1861 – 1865." I don't know who made the note on the back of the foil paper. Oscar? Or maybe Oscar's cousin Stub, another relative I had uncovered. Both served in the Union army somewhere in the south. Maybe the money was theirs.

As an adult, I understood money better than I did as a child. The Confederate bills told a sad story. The Confederacy lacked the gold or silver necessary to support their economy so they simply printed paper money with no backing. There were no coins in the collection I had discovered, but there were bills for as little as ten cents. I wondered what their economy would have been like if they had won their war and become an independent country.

The bills were old, faded, worn paper as soft and delicate as thin silk or tissue paper. The money was from many localities, mostly in Virginia though there was a dollar bill from Alabama and several from Raleigh, North Carolina. Most of the money was marked from the Confederate States of America, issued by the Capitol in Richmond. I found a ten dollar and a five dollar bill. There was one for two dollars and fifty cents and several more with less value, twenty-five cents and ten cents. There were many issued by various counties around Virginia; Bland County, Prince Edward, Wythe County, Bedford, Monroe, Greenbrier and yes, Roanoke, not far from Lynchburg.

Somehow the Confederate money came into our possession. Maybe Oscar was in a prisoner of war camp in Virginia. Maybe he did bring it home with him after the war. It might be tangible evidence that one piece of his story as related to me by my mom was true.

Still, a lot of the story didn't make sense. The unlikely story that people in Virginia knew we had the money and hated us for it was only a part of the problem. I had studied history, and I wasn't aware of any Confederate prison camps in Virginia. Mostly they were in the Deep South, in Alabama and places like Andersonville, Georgia. Maybe the money was from my father's side of the family since he was raised in Georgia. But the undeniable fact was that we had the money, and a lot of it was from Virginia. How we got it remained a mystery. The details of the story would require more research. I would learn more, all in good time.

Merlin Weighs In

THE YEAR AFTER DEBBIE and I finished the restoration of *The Flowers Personified,* my father-in-law Merlin Carr came to spend Christmas with us at our home in Rhode Island. I was eager to show him the book.

"Look at this," I said. "My great-grandfather Oscar gave this to my great-grandmother Maggie before they were married. He signed the front page 'to my friend Maggie.' And she kept it for years. She even pressed flowers in it. I don't know why the flowers were important to her. Or to him. Maybe they were from an anniversary or from their wedding or from the day he proposed. And look. There's even a four-leaf clover. Maybe they found it one day when they were on a picnic together. He gave the book to her at the end of the Civil War. It's dated Christmas, 1865."

Merlin inspected the book, his thick fingers turning the pages. "Was he in the Civil War?" he asked, his voice a resonant bass. Merlin is a Navy man. He served on the USS Spangler during the Korean War and keeps in touch with others from the Spangler's crew. Military records matter to him.

"Yes. I believe so. My mother has always told me how he ended the war in a prisoner of war camp in Virginia. We have a packet of Confederate money somewhere that she says he brought home with him after the war. When I was little growing up in Virginia, she believed that our neighbors and other people knew somehow that we had the money and thought our relatives stole it from the Confederacy. She was sure our neighbors hated us because we were Yankees."

My wife Debbie joined the conversation. "I've been researching Peter's relatives online with Google and Ancestry. It seems like Oscar was from New York State, and he was in the Civil War, but I don't know what regiment he served with."

Merlin replied, "A New York regiment. Interesting. Did he kill anybody? Was he wounded?"

"I don't know. But see the way there are flowers pressed here," I said. I was enamored with the romantic side of the book, the long-cherished keepsakes and the pressed flowers. I didn't want to know if Oscar killed anyone.

"Huh," Merlin said. "I know that some of my relatives were officers in the Civil War with New York companies. I wonder if your great-grandfather served under one of my relatives."

Merlin and Debbie are Carrs. The Carr family is all-in when it comes to family history. There is a *Carr Book*, a thick, red-covered, hard-bound book that details the family history from the Carr's first arrival in North America, following Roger Williams to Jamestown, Rhode Island, not far from where Debbie and I lived. They ran a ferry across Narragansett Bay from Jamestown to Newport. One Carr became a Colonial Governor. There is a Carr Lane on Jamestown Island, and the original Carr Homestead is midway along Carr Lane. The Carr family can trace their lineage from those early Carrs in Rhode Island almost up to the present day. Debbie is listed in the book, but it stops before she married me and our children were born. The book is stuffed with other papers; birth announcements, programs from weddings, newspaper clippings about deaths. Debbie and I might be in among those papers somewhere.

I shook my head and walked away. The thought that one of my ancestors might have been answering to orders from my wife's family was distressing. I imagined a General Carr inspecting the troops and taking my great-grandfather Oscar to task. "Stand up straight, Private McMurray! And tuck in that uniform." I heard Oscar, "Yes sir. Right away sir." I thought of him fumbling to tuck in his uniform shirt as General Carr shook his head, frowned, and marched away.

For the moment I was done with Oscar and the Civil War and General Carr. I found a football bowl game on television and sat down to watch. A college from one state was playing another college from some other state. It was a civilized form of a fight for bragging rights between rival states, unlike the Civil War. I doubted that anyone would be killed. I settled on the sofa with the game while Debbie led Merlin to the computer and explained how she did her online research for relatives. It was his first exposure to Google. She cut him loose on the internet and headed off for more Christmas cookie baking.

The game roared along on the television. Then I heard Merlin. "Huh. What in the world? Look at this. Your Oscar's regiment? It's the New York 177th. And one of his commanders was a Carr. But I don't recognize the name. This Carr must not be a relative."

I focused on the game. The score was 37-14. Somebody was winning, and the crowd was wild, their shouts almost drowning out the television announcers.

After more time Merlin called out to me. "I found him! Asa Carr. He's the one I was looking for, my relative, my family. I knew he would be here. He graduated West Point in the top half of his class and served as an officer for the rest of his life. He was out west fighting Indians in the so-called Indian Wars back before the Civil War, and he came back east to lead a company from New York when the Civil War started. But I don't believe it's your great-grandfather's regiment. And after the war he went back out west to fight the Indians again."

I continued watching the game. Merlin kept up his research about Asa Carr. Suddenly he laughed. "Ha!" he called out, triumphantly. "Well, I'll be. Asa Carr fought a battle against the Indians at a place not far from where I live now in Phoenix. He won too!"

"My great-grandfather was a brushmaker near Albany," I said. "He was an artist." On the television the game was almost over. It didn't seem important to me who won.

9

Off to Lansingburgh

DEBBIE HAD LOST A bet. She owed me an escape weekend, and she chose to take me to Albany to seek my past. We left Rhode Island on a Friday evening in late April and checked into a motel north of Albany, near Troy. The city that is now Troy once included the town of Lansingburgh, Oscar's home. Waterford, where Maggie lived, was a couple of miles away, across the Hudson River. We had done our research online. We were ready.

Saturday morning was cool with a light drizzle falling, typical springtime in upstate New York. We had leads on a few places to seek Oscar and Maggie near Troy. We knew that they had lived in Lansingburgh when they were first married. We had an address, 577 Ann Street in Troy. Google Maps revealed nothing about an Ann Street in Troy, but an address of any sort was a place to start.

We had found information about a Historical Society and Museum in Waterford. That was our first stop. We drove down a side alley around a corner to a dead-end parking lot next to the well-kept, old two-story white house that was the museum. A small, hand-lettered card on the door informed us that the museum would open to the public on the first of May, a week later.

Below the parking lot a wide park stretched to the river, a canal and a lock. I looked across a busy Escher-like maze of waterways and roadways and bridges, water flowing in channels in different directions on different levels. It was the junction of the Mohawk River, the Hudson River, and the Champlain and Erie Canals. Waterford is an economically depressed town now, but the convergence of all these waterways made it a thriving place more than a century ago. The advent of the railroad made the canals obsolete and led to the region's decline.

I couldn't come back a week later when the Historical Society would be open, and I was on a mission to find Oscar and Maggie. Time was short. I would have to look elsewhere. Debbie and I left and drove over the bridge to Troy. Lansingburgh was the northern section of the town. We tracked our way to the Lansingburgh Historical Society in a Victorian house on First Avenue near the corner of 114th Street, set among several smaller homes on the Hudson riverbank. A sign next to the house identified it as the Melville House. Herman Melville grew up here, graduated from the Lansingburgh Academy, and wrote his first two books while living in this house. Now it's the Historical Society, but it was open only by appointment and again, not at all until the first of May. I had been to two historical societies in less than an hour, both of which were closed until the following week. Oscar and Maggie had lived somewhere near here more than one hundred years ago, but I was one week too early to find them.

We still had one more possible target, an address for the Rensselaer County Historical Society in downtown Troy. Off we went. The Historical Society adjoined the historic Hart-Cluett House and Museum. It was on a quiet street in an old brick townhouse fronting on a brick-paved sidewalk. Trees with new leaves gave a speckled shade as the sun fought to break out of the overcast. We parked across from the townhouse and walked up the stone steps to the door. It was locked. But a sign stated that it was open on Saturdays at 1:00 p.m. It was almost noon. We had time to find a place for lunch and come back. The rain abated, and the sun began to shine.

Several blocks up the street was the Illium Café, a crowded restaurant with a diverse menu catering to the college crowd from Rensselaer Polytech, several blocks away. The food was excellent, and we lingered, checking our time, waiting for 1:00 p.m.

Then we returned to the Historical Society. A woman greeted us inside the door near a table where she sold tickets for the house tours and gave away brochures. She listened patiently as we described our reason for being there.

"You don't want to tour the Hart-Cluett House? You want to check genealogy? That's upstairs. Go on up. Take the elevator. Larry will meet you." She dialed Larry's number on her telephone as we waited for the elevator.

Larry was waiting when the elevator doors opened on the second floor. He was a small, crew-cut man, perhaps fifty years old. Suspenders supported his blue jeans. He wore a yellow oxford dress shirt with the collar tabs buttoned down, a bow tie, and hiking boots. His greeting was a simple "Hello."

"You're Larry?"

"Yes." He gave a slight smile and adjusted his glasses.

"We want to track down my great-grandfather and grandmother. The woman downstairs told us you might be able to help."

"I expect. Do you have anything to start with?"

"Yes. Their names were Oscar McMurray or maybe MacMurray. And Maggie Teachout. He's from Lansingburgh. She's from Waterford. They lived back in the mid-1800s. We think they lived at 577 Ann Street, but I can't find anything about an Ann Street in Troy or Lansingburgh."

"Let me see what I can do."

Larry led us into a cluster of rooms on the second floor at the front of the old building. "You can work here. Give me a moment to get you started." He set us up at a wide table and walked away.

We looked around. The room was surprisingly ornate for a research space. A thick but worn oriental rug covered the floor beneath the table. A gilt-framed mirror hung on one wall. The room was dominated by books on shelves, cabinets, drawers, and card files.

In graduate school I had done a lot of historical research, reading primary sources, letters, and other papers from Jefferson and Adams, giving insight into the evolutions of their political philosophies. I found research tedious but necessary to learn about the past. I had chosen education rather than pure history as a career after graduate school but now I was deep into the research again, this time with a personal motive.

People were working silently in the space around us. I asked one man what he was looking for. He explained that he was from nearby Sage College and was there to upgrade the Historical Society computer system. He seemed disinterested in the people doing historical research. There was another man, bearded, middle aged, with a dark ponytail. He wore a plain red t-shirt, baggy shorts, and a Mets cap. He was sorting through old newspapers. He too was seeking his family roots. An elderly couple was picking up a manila envelope filled with papers Larry had prepared for them.

The old couple shook Larry's hand and turned to the elevator. Larry came back, checked some files, opened a wide flat drawer, and sorted through a stack of maps. He called to me. "Mid-1800s you said? Ann Street? I've got it."

He placed some map books and three flat maps on the table in front of me. "They changed the old street names around the turn of the century," he explained. "It was the 'modern thing to do,' numbering the streets. You can reference Ann Street on the old maps to the new numbered street maps from around 1900. Those street numbers match today's maps."

Comparing two maps, one with street names, the other with numbers, it was easy to see that Ann Street was now 6th Avenue. Finding 577 was more of a challenge. Larry stood by silently, hands clasped in front of him, watching me work. Finally he spoke, pointing to a vast map, three feet wide and six feet long, that covered the table. "This one is from around 1850, maybe 1860. It shows the lot numbers. I don't see a number 577 on Ann Street. But there are numbers 575 and 576 right up near Canal Street. Canal Street is now 120th. So your great-grandfather's house might be in that vicinity. But it's not showing up on the lot plan."

He paused for a moment and then abruptly raised an index finger, a gesture that suggested he had a new thought. He turned without a word and hurried off to another map drawer. He came back with a more modern map. "This might help. They put up house numbers in the 1870s, I believe. This map shows those new house numbers from the 1920s. They don't match the lot numbers. See what you can find."

He left me to the new map. 577 Sixth Avenue was near 115th Street, several houses before 116th Street. It was only a few blocks away from Herman Melville's house on First at 114th. I wondered for a moment if the Melville's and the McMurray's knew each other. Bingo! I had a location for Oscar and Maggie's house.

Larry came back with more books, some opened and stacked to mark the places he had found to be significant. "Oscar McMurray? I've found him. Yes, he lived at 577 Ann Street at least until 1884, but you already know that. His father James lived there for a while as well, but he seems to have left in the 1860s. They both worked for Van Kleeck's Brushmaking here in Lansingburgh. The brushmaking business moved to a factory in Waterford in 1864 during the Civil War. That would have been a hard time for businesses, but perhaps Van Kleeck's took the slow time as an opportunity to consolidate the brushmaking from a cottage industry into a single factory that became available at that time."

He opened another book and pointed to a listing. "Oscar and Maggie appear to have attended the First Presbyterian Church of Lansingburgh. That's gone now, but it was only a few blocks from their house. I don't find a record from Lansingburgh for their marriage at that church. Maybe they got married in Waterford.

"Here's his Civil War record. The New York 177th. The records call the war a Rebellion until 1863 which is when he was in the war. They begin calling it a Civil War or a Revolution in later records. There are other records and information from that time, documenting other regiments from this region. But he was in the 177th. They served in 1863 on the Mississippi River. They were assisting Sherman with his attack on Vicksburg. The record shows that Oscar came home to Lansingburgh in September 1863. He was gone for less than a year. It was what they call a nine-month regiment. He was lucky. A lot of the 177th didn't make it home."

Wait a minute, I thought, suddenly confused. Oscar served on the Mississippi? My mother told me he was in a prisoner of war camp in Virginia till the end of the war. What about that Confederate money from Virginia she showed me? And he was out by September 1863? These are the facts, documented by the records of the 177th regiment. Where did my mother's story about her grandfather come from? And how did we get that Confederate money? Was none of my mother's account of his Civil War service true?

It took me several minutes to digest these facts. Oscar was never in Virginia during the war. He was out of the military and back in Lansingburgh long before the end. It was unlikely he was in a prisoner of war camp if he was home in less than a year. Mom had told me how he burned his uniform because it was full of bugs when he came home. Could I still believe even this detail about his time in the war? I needed to research and rethink everything about Oscar's service if the fundamental fact of his prisoner of war status in Virginia was untrue.

I discovered several more interesting facts about Oscar and his family. He and Maggie served as witnesses to the marriage of Addie E. McMurray to Rollo D. Comstock on September 28, 1865. I assumed that Addie must be a relative. This event when Oscar and Maggie were together was still three months before he gave her *The Flowers Personified*. I found very few references to their friends, James Eddy and Lottie Sweeney, who witnessed their wedding in 1867.

Oscar's mother Hannah died on June 27, 1866. She was born in Canada, but Oscar's grandfather Robert was born in Lansingburgh in 1798. So the McMurray family was in Lansingburgh long before Oscar and Maggie's time. Oscar's father James remarried Hannah's younger sister Sarah the year after Hannah died. They moved to St. Paul, Minnesota. He died there in 1888. Newlyweds Oscar and Maggie remained in the house on Ann Street where their children were born and raised. They all moved to Vailsburg, New Jersey, possibly in the late 1880s. They were certainly there by 1900.

The story was becoming clear, gaps filling in. Old truths about my family were now proven false. A new chronicle of Oscar and Maggie's life was emerging.

I thanked Larry for his help, took copies of key documents and left. On the way back to the motel I travelled north through Troy, back into what was once Lansingburgh. I found Sixth Avenue and drove, my excitement building, checking the numbers on the houses, seeking 577. On the left, just past 115th Street we found it, a small, simple clapboard house with a side entrance. The foundation was old fieldstone, painted gray. It had new vinyl siding. A chain link fence surrounded it with a gate opened in the back to a school on an adjoining lot. The house had probably less than 1,000 square feet of living space but this was where Oscar and Maggie lived, where their children, including my grandfather James, were born.

I have roots. I have a home. At last I know where I come from.

I snapped a picture of the house, self-conscious and afraid of intruding on the lives of the people who now lived there. It was only a moment, but it was a landmark in my life where, until then, I had so little certainty about my heritage.

The next morning, we returned to Troy for Sunday brunch at the Illium Cafe. As we ate, I tried to imagine Troy and Lansingburgh as my home town. Yes, there was a house there where my roots might be found. But it was from a remote time. Generations had passed since Oscar and Maggie moved to New Jersey. The people who must live in that house now have no connection to me.

Several years later, after my mom had passed away, Debbie and I found the last home where Oscar and Maggie lived in Vailsburg, New Jersey on Richelieu Terrace. We were driving north from Virginia for a vacation with friends in New England. Following computerized directions, we turned off the Garden State Parkway at exit 144 and began pushing west with the traffic and the stop lights, through Newark on South Orange Avenue.

Newark has changed from the bustling enterprising town it must have been at the beginning of the twentieth century. Dirt streets are now paved. Vailsburg Park is still there on the south side of the avenue, with a wrought iron arch set on brick posts at the entrance and paths, now asphalt, through grass and trees. But today, many of the stores and houses along South Orange Avenue are run down. Some of the shops are empty and boarded up. Stores that are still in business often have metal grates over the windows. The region has become hard, not the way I imagine it was more than one hundred years ago when the community was new. Streets are congested with traffic. It is noisy and crowded with people along the sidewalks, waiting for busses, chatting with each other.

Richelieu Terrace is a mile west of the Garden State Parkway on the south side of South Orange Avenue. It is a quiet neighborhood with less activity than several blocks back, closer to Newark. The McMurray home, 32 Richelieu Terrace, is a large, wide house, three stories high and deep, running back from the street. The yard is fenced, and other houses crowd close by on either side, separated only by narrow driveways. There is a community center across the street that appears to have been a church in an earlier time. Could that have been Oscar and Maggie's church?

I got out of my car to take a picture of the house. While I was on the street a teenage boy and his mother left a neighboring house and got in a car. They drove away before I could ask them about the house or the community center. They appeared disinterested in me as I stood in the street photographing the house next to theirs.

Maplewood, where James settled and where my mom grew up, is only a few miles to the south of Richelieu Terrace. I remember visiting there when I was a boy. It was less crowded and more tree-lined than Vailsburg.

Debbie's father Merlin Carr was born and raised on a farm outside Miller, South Dakota. The farm and the farmhouse are still in the Carr family. Debbie's cousins still live there and work in downtown Miller. She has taken me to Miller and the farm and shown me places where she played when she visited as a child. I have heard the stories about the original soddy the family built on that same property near Turtle Creek. That is a real family homestead. I felt an attachment to the little house on Sixth Avenue, Ann Street, but it was not really the homestead I had hoped to find. Neither was the Vailsburg house.

I wished that I could have shared the story of my trip to Lansingburgh and Troy with my mother. But maybe she already knew about the house in Lansingburgh, maybe even about the one in Vailsburg. It's possible she was born in the Vailsburg house. Maybe she was relating to me the fabricated stories of her father James. Her defensiveness and anger around the Irish question might have been proof she already knew the truth that we weren't Scottish or any of the other misinformation she had shared with me. I never told my mother that we found Oscar and Maggie's home in Lansingburgh. To do so would have been to confess to her that I was still seeking my roots and that would bring up the whole Irish or Scottish debate.

Questions Following
Lansingburgh

I WAS SATISFIED BY my discoveries in Lansingburgh. I had found the house where Oscar and Maggie had lived. My grandfather was born there. I now knew about the Van Kleeck brushmaking business. I understood the proximity of Lansingburgh to Waterford and could understand how Oscar and Maggie might have met.

But I was bothered by so many new questions. In the days after my visit to Lansingburgh I puzzled over all the information I had uncovered.

What about the Civil War records? I had always believed my mother's story that Oscar had served throughout the war and had been in a prison camp in Virginia at the end. We had that Confederate money. If Mom was wrong, how did we get that money? But the records in Lansingburgh had him serving in the New York 177th Volunteer regiment. And that unit served for less than a year on the Mississippi. I had brought home a few notes about the regiment and could now do some online searches to learn more.

I also had a dark photocopy of a newspaper article about the glorious return to Lansingburgh of the New York 2nd Volunteer regiment. They had been gone for two years, coming home shortly before Oscar mustered out of his service with the 177th. I needed to learn more about the 2nd regiment to understand the world that Oscar and Maggie lived in at that time. And I had learned at the Historical Society that Oscar's uncle Sylvester McMurray had been in the 123rd regiment. What did the 123rd do during the war? All these bits of Civil War history demanded more research.

It seemed clear that my heritage was Irish McMurray, but not Catholic. Oscar and Maggie attended a Presbyterian church in Lansingburgh and were married in a Methodist church in Waterford. And, small as the McMurray house on Ann Street was, there seemed to be a lot of McMurrays living there over the years. Census records disclosed a tight community of brushmakers in Lansingburgh, several of them McMurrays. Aside from the brushmaking there were lots of other McMurrays for me to investigate.

Who were James Eddy and Lottie Sweeney? There was evidence that they lived in the area, but I could find nothing about them except that they witnessed Oscar and Maggie's wedding.

Oscar's father married his wife's sister Sarah in Ohio shortly after his first wife Hannah died. And they left for the frontier of the Midwest shortly after the wedding. Why? And why did Oscar and Maggie take their family to New Jersey in the mid-1880s? Why would they leave the town where they had lived their whole lives, leave his job at Van Kleecks and move more than one hundred miles? I had questions. But I also had clues, new leads that would help me continue my search for my family.

Other names were beginning to appear. There were Addie McMurray, Sylvester McMurray, and maybe someone named Charlotte. I needed to learn more about Sylvester. How closely was he connected to Oscar and Maggie, and what was his story? Who was Addie? And what about her husband Rollo Comstock?

I began to do more research with Debbie's help. I Googled names and found more information. Debbie worked with Ancestry.com. Ancestry was helpful but filled with confusing information. Other relatives, doing their own research, added records that were not always accurate. It didn't help that there were several families named McMurray living in the Troy region. And most of them were brushmakers. I didn't know if they were loosely related.

Digging through all the records my family began to emerge. Sylvester, Addie, Charlotte, and one or two others were siblings of James, Oscar's father. They all lived in Lansingburgh and were a very close family. At times, the census records I reviewed in the Rensselaer Historical Society showed several of them sharing the house on Ann Street with their brother James and their nephew Oscar. Oscar appeared to be very close to his Uncle Sylvester. Oscar and Maggie were witnesses at Addie's wedding to Rollo Comstock.

Oscar and Maggie had three children while living in Lansingburgh: Carrie, Eugene, and James, my grandfather. These are accounted for in census records for Lansingburgh. The Teachout family Bible shows they had another child much later, Edna, who only lived a few months.

Slowly I began to build a family tree. It became a document that I updated each time I uncovered a new fact.

11

Battlefields

THERE ARE TWO KINDS of National and State Parks; natural wonders and historic sites. The natural wonders are places like the Grand Canyon, the Cape Cod National Seashore and, here in Virginia, several spots in the Blue Ridge Mountains. Historic sites are frequently Revolutionary War or Civil War battlefields that typically include overgrown bunkers, earthworks, and wide meadows where thousands of men died. There are short educational films to watch in visitors' centers. Outside are cannons, weathered and corroded black or green, placed where the battle lines used to be.

I don't often go to battlefields. They make me uncomfortable. I sometimes feel the ghosts of the dead. Despite my fears I have been to my share. Yorktown, where the last battle in the Revolutionary War was fought, isn't far from where I live. Ghosts or not, it's a place I had to see.

I had visited several notable Civil War battlefields before I began researching the lives of Oscar and his Uncle Sylvester, nicknamed Stub, and their involvement in that war. I had been to Gettysburg and seen the rolling fields and woodlands with the arrayed statues commemorating the regiments that fought there. A docent rode with me and Debbie in my car around the expanse of the Gettysburg battlefield, detailing the actions of that multi-day battle. I was appalled at the number of casualties on both sides. I had also toured Vicksburg, getting a sense of that pivotal battle, fought on the same days as Gettysburg a thousand miles to the south.

Now my research had informed me that Sylvester, Uncle Stub, had been at Gettysburg and Oscar had been involved right down the Mississippi River from Vicksburg. Where else might they have fought in the war? There were suggestions that Stub and possibly Oscar might have been at Fredericksburg and Chancellorsville in Virginia. That could explain the Virginia Confederate dollars. I had to know. I had to go.

Fredericksburg, Chancellorsville, and The Wilderness battlefields are separated by a few miles. Today they are on either side of interstate 95, a distance north of the Confederate capital of Richmond that a nineteenth century army could march in a few days. The fighting began in December 1862 as the Union army approached and attempted to cross the Rappahannock River at Fredericksburg. They set up one of their headquarters at Chatham Manor, a brick mansion on the north shore of the river, and converted the mansion to a hospital when the fighting began. The Confederate army defended from high ground south of the town, setting their artillery on a ridge, Marye's Heights, and placing their infantry behind a rock wall in the natural trench of a sunken road.

It took a day for the Union army to fight their way across the river and through the streets of Fredericksburg. Over the next days they kept trying to advance, futilely assaulting Marye's Heights. The Union soldiers marched across an open meadow, charging uphill. Confederate artillery rained down on them. As they got closer, infantry in the sunken road picked them off. This initial fighting ended in a stalemate with the Confederate forces controlling the ridge and the Union troops camped back across the river.

As spring approached in 1863, the Union made a second attempt, fighting again at Fredericksburg and trying an end run to the west at Chancellorsville. The fighting spread into a heavily forested area known as The Wilderness. The Union succeeded briefly in taking Marye's Heights but was beaten back at Chancellorsville. It was possibly the most successful day of the war for the rebels, though they lost General Stonewall Jackson to friendly fire. The Confederate army under Robert E. Lee was encouraged by this victory and began to push the Union forces back. Lee's advance finally ended two months later at Gettysburg.

I began my tour of this horrific battleground by visiting Chatham Manor. It's a beautiful, old brick mansion with a formal garden at the entrance. Twentieth century owners of the house built the garden, but during the war, when the house served as a hospital for the Union troops, the same ground became a graveyard. One war-time description of Chatham Manor described amputated limbs piled under a catalpa tree that still stands in front of the house. The river side of the house gives an open view across the Rappahannock River to old Fredericksburg. Three graves of unknown Union soldiers are still on the property there, above the river, set among the obligatory cannons.

I met two National Park Service volunteers in the lobby of the house. One, named James Padgett, began to narrate his standard story about the house. I allowed a brief history from Padgett and then interrupted. "I'm researching the story of two of my relatives who might have served here," I said.

"Really? What regiments were they in? What were their names? I can look them up for you."

"My great-grandfather was Oscar McMurray. He was in the New York 177th. That was a nine-month regiment, but I believe he served on the Mississippi, not here. His uncle was named Sylvester McMurray. He was in the New York 123rd. He's more likely to have been here."

Padgett set to work checking files on a computer. The other volunteer was less interested and not particularly excited by my request. "Union regiments you're looking for," he said with a hint of disdain. "You know that General Lee's army held off the Yankees at Fredericksburg and won at Chancellorsville."

"Yes. I know. I've got ties on both sides," I replied, trying to win him over. "My middle name is Gordon. That's also my son's middle name and my grandson's. I got the name from my father and grandfather. They're from Georgia. The Gordon middle name comes from a General Gordon from Georgia. Our family story has it that General Gordon was Lee's Aide de Camp."

"Oh yes. General Gordon. I believe I've heard of him. He would have been here alongside General Lee." The second volunteer seemed to be appeased.

Padgett spoke up. "I've found Sylvester. Yes, the New York 123rd was here. They fought in the first assault on Marye's Heights and spent the winter in Stafford County. Then they were heavily involved over in Chancellorsville. I don't find a record of your Uncle Sylvester McMurray being wounded or killed here."

"No. I know that he survived the war. He went on to Gettysburg and was in the war right to the end."

"Good. Let me do some more research. I'll email you anything else I find. Why don't you go on with your tour of the house and the battlefields?"

I thanked Padgett, gave him my email address, shook his hand, and went out.

After walking the grounds of Chatham Manor, I drove across the river into old Fredericksburg. I went through the town to the battlefield, parked, and followed a marked walking trail from the National Park Visitor Center along the sunken road. I imagined what it would have been like to be a Rebel soldier looking down the slope from behind the natural protection of the road and the rock wall. Now I saw houses, streets with parked cars, and utility poles. During the battle it was an open field with few trees offering cover. Rebel soldiers would have been firing straight into ranks of Union soldiers struggling out of breath as they advanced up the incline.

Climbing to Marye's Heights, I was struck again by the natural protection given by the elevation. I thought of the artillery set here, firing down the hill right into the massed Union army regiments. Now, more than 150 years later, the only sound I heard was the soft pock of tennis balls being volleyed on the University of Mary Washington tennis courts behind a grove of trees. I walked from Marye's Heights a short distance to the Fredericksburg National Cemetery where the remains of more than 15,000 of the dead from the months of fighting are buried. Less than 3,000 have been identified. The rest have simple markers with numbers, no names, their identities lost.

That evening when I got home I had an email from Mr. Padgett. He sent me a link to a letter a Major James C. Rogers, an officer in the 123rd, sent back to his hometown newspaper, the *Sandy Hill Herald* in New York, describing their action at Chancellorsville. In part, the letter read:

Suffice it for the present, to say, that the 123d has done honor to itself and its friends at home, and that its praise are on the lips of all who were witnesses of, or have heard of its gallantry. In the great fight at Chancellorsville, Sunday, May 3, it (the New York 123rd) was in the frontline, its right resting on the plank road, of which Jackson's corps advanced to the attack, and they were under the most terrific fire of Artillery and Infantry that the engines of the war ever poured upon men, with shells from our own batteries massed on the hill behind us, and the enemies in front crashing and splintering the trees, and tearing the ground all around it, and bursting in its ranks, and with minie balls like the swarming of bees sweeping thro and about it, the regiment coolly stood its ground, as though all this were an everyday exercise, and the air were not crowded with the missiles of death, and the moments fraught with the destinies of a nation and laden with the dying gasp of countless of her bravest sons. The regiment was put into position at 3 a.m., and immediately with what tools it could get, it commenced constructing a kind of defense along its front of fallen trees and brush, which was not by any means finished, when at sunrise the battle began in twice in the heat of the contest did the Rebels with fiendish yells charge in solid columns directly up upon this breastwork. But the storm of grape and canister and bursting shells from our batteries, which plowed the ground along our fraught come in the murderous volleys from the muskets of our men, nothing mortal could withstand. And soon besides a number of prisoners and the heaps of dead and wounded, scattered graybacks running for dear life, though the woods to the rear, was all that was left of those compact columns that came so dauntlessly up to the assault.

I thought of Major Rogers sending the letter to brag about his regiment's valor. But I also imagined the families of the soldiers in the 123rd reading his account and knowing the ultimate losing outcome of the battle, worrying about their loved ones. How many men from the 123rd rest in unmarked graves in that cemetery on the hill in Fredericksburg?

From my research, I knew the long, storied saga of the 123rd New York regiment. There was Uncle Stub, surviving this battle and going on to Gettysburg, and continuing down to join Sherman in Alabama and Georgia. For Stub, this bloody encounter was just one of many deadly days during his tour.

Homecoming:
May 1863

PRAISE THE LORD! THE people of Troy got the news that the Second New York Volunteer Regiment was coming home. The local newspapers had chronicled the battles won and lost, but the personal accounts of the plight of the men from Troy were rarely reported. It was known that the men who died in battle were buried in mass graves near the site of the fight. Often the men could not be identified and were buried in simple graves with no name, just a number. Many of the people of Troy didn't know for sure if their loved ones were among the dead. Everyone assumed that their family members were on the way home since there was so little news from the front to make them think otherwise.

The Troy town fathers planned to make May 14, 1863 the most glorious day in the history of the city. They set aside more than $1,500, the price of a small house, to fund the celebration. Planning for the welcome home ceremonies took weeks. The parade route was laid out to stretch for more than a mile, winding around blocks through the city from Steamboat Landing on the Hudson River to Washington Square. The committee preparing the welcome celebration built a wooden triumphal arch in the park, modeled after the one they had seen in the pictures from Paris. It was decorated with flags, bunting, garlands of evergreen and wreaths. Behind the arch, the city erected a low platform from which dignitaries would give speeches.

Families of the returning soldiers met the steamer Chauncey Vanderbilt when it arrived at the dock at sunrise after cruising up the river overnight from New York City. Parents and wives stood near the dock, calling out the names of their men, scanning the crowd of weary soldiers walking down the boat ramp. When they saw them, they greeted their men with jubilant hugs and tearful embraces. They helped them fall in for the march behind the long parade that had assembled near the dock at dawn.

Some of the families who had not already learned that their men were dead received this tragic news on the dock. Other families were met with the disturbing information that their men were alive but unable to travel. These men were still in hospitals in Virginia or Washington. The families of the dead and of the hospitalized soldiers who had not returned abandoned the parade and stayed at the landing numb, sharing each other's grief.

A few of the returning soldiers were unable to march because of their wounds. The parade organizers assisted these men to carriages so they could ride along the parade route behind their regiment. All of the families of the survivors gathered behind the end of the parade, ready to follow their soldiers to Washington Square.

Every civic organization had a contingent in the parade. Fire brigades from each district, the Troy Young Men's Association, and various trade associations, marched at the front of the parade. There were five brass bands, notably the locally famous bands, Dorings and Sullivans. Houses throughout the city were decked with flags. Crowds lined both sides of the roads for the length of the parade route and filled Washington Square behind the wooden triumphal arch. The cheering was incessant as the parade marched by. The Female Seminary students cheered loudest of all and showered the returning soldiers with bouquets. Instructions printed in the newspaper requested that the reception should be enthusiastic but decorous. In spite of this, celebratory cannons were fired, something that had been explicitly forbidden. The citizens could not contain their excitement.

Maggie went to Washington Square to await the parade. She hoped against hope that Oscar and the 177th regiment would also be mustered out and he too would be coming home to her, meeting her on this sun-filled happy day. He still had three months left to serve. Even if Oscar wouldn't be home yet she couldn't stay away from the event. All of Troy, Lansingburgh, and Waterford had taken the day as a holiday. No schools or businesses were open. The whole town turned out to greet their heroes.

She was surprised to learn that the parade route had been changed at the last moment. There was a sudden, unexplained need to cut it short. It would take detours, eliminating the original circuits around some of the city blocks. The route had also been planned to circle Washington Square at the end with the soldiers finishing at the reviewing stand. Word went through the crowd that it would simply stop at the reviewing stand without circling the park. The soldiers would stand in their ranks there. These changes did nothing to dampen the joyous mood

Maggie pushed through the noisy crowd, gathering her wide skirt close to her, and positioned herself where she could have the best view of the returning heroes when they stopped at the park. She could see the bands and the civic organizations in Troy any other time. Today was the day for the soldiers, and she wanted to be as close as possible to them when they arrived.

She first heard the distant drumming, echoing through the town as the parade approached. Then from several blocks away she heard the cheering crowd and the music from the marching bands. At last the parade was in sight. Her anticipation built as ranks of civic leaders and fire companies marched past.

Finally the soldiers appeared. They marched heads down, shuffling, many with their eyes focused anywhere but on the crowd. Maggie was shocked by how small the regiment had become. She remembered the 400 men who had marched away so smartly just two years ago. Now less than half were returning. Behind the marching soldiers came a line of carriages carrying the wounded. She was appalled to see that some were missing limbs, with bandaged stumps visible as they sat and reclined in their carriages.

Maggie had read the newspaper reports that Colonel Park had been wounded at Chancellorsville, one of the last battles fought by the New York Second Regiment. He and a number of others were still in hospitals in Washington. But the soldiers who had returned were certainly deserving of the hero's welcome they were receiving. Maggie pulled her skirt in and slipped through to the front edge of the crowd to be closer to these brave young men. She reached out to touch a soldier on the sleeve as he stood at attention in his rank next to the reviewing platform, but he pulled away distracted and wouldn't look at her. As close as Maggie was to the ranks of soldiers, she could smell the men, a rancid smell of wet wool, sweat, and another feral smell she couldn't describe.

The cheering continued, growing louder, the crowd feeding on the thrill of seeing their returning soldiers. Mayor VanAlstyne stood at the front of the small stage with a thick sheaf of papers in his hand. He waved for the crowd to become quiet. After some time, it did. He began reading his speech, calling out poetic words in a voice that reached everyone in the crowded square.

He traced the history of the Second New York Volunteer Regiment from its formation, recalling the muster day two years earlier, citing the bravery of the men before him. He detailed its record, its time at Fort Monroe, its involvement at so many battles big and small, Malvern Hill, Fredericksburg, and lastly at Chancellorsville. It was a long speech, but he knew these men were worthy of nothing less.

The Mayor continued, speaking for the citizens of Troy but addressing the soldiers.

> *It is, of course, apparent to us, as it is doubtless more fully apparent to you, that you return with thinned ranks. You left behind you, beneath unfriendly soil, and unmarked by any token of affection and remembrance, many of your noble comrades; others who left with you in health and vigor are now lingering with wounds received in battle and are perhaps never to know perfect health again. Among them may be named your recent worthy commanding officer, Colonel Park. Such are the melancholy incidents of war; such the sacrifices that wicked men, in armed rebellion to the Government, called you and us to make.*

As he finished this statement he was stunned to see a soldier on the front line slump to one knee and then sit on the ground. The Mayor still had several pages to read but he concluded quickly and handed the proceedings over to Lieutenant Colonel Olmstead, a local hero who had assumed command in Colonel Park's absence. Olmstead spoke briefly, his voice weak, thanking the mayor and the town. He then directed the parade to conclude by marching the short remaining distance across the park to the Courthouse where the Second Regiment was to be dismissed.

Maggie saw Oscar's family in the crowd after the parade dispersed. "Good day isn't it?" she greeted them, infusing her voice with cheeriness. "What did you think of the festivities?"

Oscar's father answered, his voice somber. "Yes, it's a good day. It's good that these men are back. I hope and pray that Oscar returns in a few months safe and unharmed." Maggie could read on his face that he shared her increased concern for Oscar's well-being.

This was not a time for more pleasantries and small talk. Maggie nodded, wished the McMurrays good day, and turned to begin her way back to Waterford. She walked home alone after the parade, anxious, her thinking panicky, disturbed by what she had just witnessed. On the one hand there was the parade, the bands, the crowds cheering, all of the flags and bunting. That was the excitement she had anticipated. On the other there was the battered, head-down look of the small regiment of returning soldiers. She remembered the one man sagging to the ground during Mayor VanAlstyne's interminable speech. The reality of war finally began to erode her idealism.

She thought of Oscar and worried that he hadn't come home today, though he wasn't expected. She made herself believe that he couldn't be in the same condition as the men she had just seen. But could he be that way too? He was still somewhere at war. She had only received two letters from him. Maggie prayed for him again that night, kissing his picture as she always did. But, haunted by what she had seen that morning in Washington Square, she couldn't fall asleep. She had too many sleepless nights with Oscar gone.

Maggie followed the news of the Second Regiment in the following days. She heard the story of the Quartermaster, a Lieutenant Shear. He was a noted citizen, a proper gentleman married to a prominent woman in town, and he returned to her a hero. But he had spent the days since he came home drinking heavily in local saloons, getting in fights with people, and alarming his friends with his dissipation. Colonel Olmstead interceded and sent him to a hastily established military infirmary to rest and recover. On May 29, fifteen days after the celebration in Washington Square, while still in the infirmary, Lieutenant Shear sliced his throat from ear to ear and bled to death.

Maggie also heard of a small band of veterans of the Second who met regularly in saloons to plan how they would reenlist. Over their drinks they bragged about the good life in the army and debated whether to return to the war as artillerymen or in the cavalry. Some citizens of Troy encouraged them to make their noble return to the war. Their families discouraged it.

Maggie wondered what Oscar would be like when he came home. She marked the days that remained before his anticipated return and waited for his letters.

September 24, 1863

Four months later, on September 10, Oscar was mustered out in Albany. He was not finally discharged until September 24. He came home to no fanfare. The town seemed to have had its fill of heroism and parades after its welcome for the Second. Oscar crossed the river to Steamboat Landing, walked to his house alone, folded his uniform, put it away in a drawer, bathed, and ate supper with his family. They talked quietly, tactfully avoiding any discussion of the war. Then he went to bed, desperate to see Maggie but too tired to leave his house. He slept until noon the next day.

That next afternoon, now wearing fresh clothes for the first time in months, he sat in the riverbank park on a spread blanket with Maggie. A picnic basket she had prepared sat next to them with a jug of lemonade and the remains of their late-lunch sandwiches. Indian summer sun bathed them.

Oscar was quiet, more subdued than she remembered him from before he left for the war. Maggie saw that he was thinner, with a hard look to his face. She reached to him and traced the small new mustache that curled around the corners of his mouth. "I like the mustache. It suits you. When did you grow it?"

"While I was away. It wasn't always possible to shave. I was all whiskers for a time. Now that I'm home I've cleaned up but I kept the mustache. I'm glad you like it."

She touched his hand. "What was it like?"

Oscar looked at her, and for a moment he didn't speak. She waited. He pulled his hand away and picked up a twig off the grass beside him, broke it in half, and threw the pieces into the dark river water that flowed by in front of them.

For a moment the horror of the war came back to Oscar. He had seen men get shot, seen the holes ripped into their bodies. He had smelled the blood and the burnt gunpowder and flesh. He had smelled the infections of the wounded men lying in the dirt after a battle. He had heard the screams. He could never forget the screams or the visions of the dying men, their faces taut with pain as they saw the end rushing at them.

Finally he sighed and turned to look at her.

"You can't begin to imagine what it was like," he said. "It was awful. We were on the Mississippi River in Louisiana. Even in the winter down there it was hot, as hot as summer is here. And when spring came it was unbearable. We had some little battles. Skirmishes they called them. But mostly we just sat on the Mississippi riverbank in a camp, patrolling to make sure that nothing could get through to Vicksburg up the river a ways. That's where the real fighting happened, up at Vicksburg. We had a place called Port Hudson under siege for all of June. A few days longer, I think."

"Were you ever in a big battle?" asked Maggie.

"Yes, of course."

"What was it like?" Maggie repeated. She had seen the haunted looks on the faces of the Second Regiment and she remembered the Quartermaster who committed suicide after he came home. Oscar didn't have the look of those men, but he seemed more somber than she remembered. She prayed that he hadn't been damaged too.

"It was terrifying. I have never been so scared. I saw men get shot." His voice broke. He couldn't look at her as he talked.

That was all Oscar said. He couldn't say any more about it. Not even with Maggie. He wouldn't have her know his hell. It was bad enough that each night there were the dreams. Now, sitting in the peaceful quiet, enjoying the sunlight on the riverbank with Maggie, he remembered the attack on Port Hudson.

I heard their screams. Some were killed outright. I watched them suddenly die, men I'd had breakfast with just hours before. Just like that they fell, and they're dead. It was a small number really who died in the fighting. I saw a report that said only two of our officers and seven men died from getting shot. A few were killed on the spot during our charge. More of them died later from their wounds. They'd survive the battle but then they'd take them in the medical tent, and we'd hear them screaming, and when they came out they'd have bandages where they should have had an arm or leg. They died a few days later from infections.

Oscar looked at Maggie. She begged him, "I need to know more. I have to know what you went through down there."

He replied with a touch of anger in his voice. "I can't talk about it. I won't. I watched men die. You don't want to know, and I don't want to talk about it."

Maggie went pale. She felt nauseous. He was right. She couldn't imagine what it must have been like. She squeezed his hand and waited to see if he would continue, hoping he wouldn't.

"You don't have to tell me this if you don't want to," Maggie said. She sat back, folding her hands on her skirt and faced Oscar directly. "But I love you, and I'm here for you. I want to help you."

They sat together in the stillness by the water, Maggie wondering what had happened, Oscar trying not to think about it again. But now he couldn't forget.

We rarely got really close to the enemy. Just a couple of little battles and then the two assaults on Port Hudson at the start of the siege. I always stayed as close to the ground as I could when the fighting started. It was hard when we attacked Port Hudson because I had to be standing upright, being right out there marching toward the rebels while they shot at us.

Maggie said nothing, sitting very still, watching him, reading the pale terror on his lined face.

We lost those men in the battles. The two officers and seven regulars. I still see each one of them, plain as day, the way they were before they got shot. But we lost many more to illnesses. They say we lost three more officers and 149 regular soldiers to dysentery. That's 161 men who didn't make it back from the 400 we started with. I knew we lost a lot of men, but I checked that report because I wanted to see for myself just how many there were. I needed to know.

Gently, Maggie probed again. "Were you hurt? You weren't shot, were you?"

"No. But I was sick. There was a lot of illness."

"What do you mean illness?"

"Mostly dysentery. A few other things. I got sick several times. I think it was from eating bad food or drinking bad water. And I got sick from the heat in the summer. But I'm here now. Let's forget about it."

"What's dysentery?"

Oscar looked out at the river again. He considered how he should describe it to Maggie. He must be delicate when telling her. Again she waited. "It's an intestinal disease," he said. "Probably from drinking the water. I don't know how I can talk about it in terms for a lady to hear."

"No, tell me. I want to know everything that happened to you."

Oscar focused on the river flowing in front of them and spoke slowly, deliberately. "I can't," he said, his voice firm. Again he was filled with the memories, the nightmares.

The intestinal pain and dehydration. Everyone in camp got sick with it. We're all lying around as weak as babies, and the whole camp smelled terribly. After about a week some of the men felt better. But some, particularly if it was the second time they got it, they'd just become so weak, so dehydrated, they'd die. I got it. Everyone did. I got it maybe twice. We always worried about the river water but we drank it anyway. There was one time. I was very hot and filthy dirty and I needed a bath, and the river was right there. The Mississippi is this really big river much wider than the Hudson here. It's muddy, but I needed a bath and it was a terribly hot day, so I went for a swim. I must have swallowed some water while I was swimming. I came out and got dressed again and felt cool and refreshed after being in the water. Two days later I had terrible stomach cramps and, well... the diarrhea. Unstoppable diarrhea. I slept in my tent for two days except for when, well..."

"All right," said Maggie. "You don't have to tell me. I understand."

"No you don't, but you know enough. Probably the only way we finally took control of the whole Mississippi is that the rebels were suffering worse than we were. Their camp at Port Hudson was sicker than ours. War's certainly not the romantic thing everyone wants it to be."

"I thank God that you're home. That's all behind you now."

Oscar laughed suddenly. "That's right. It's all behind me now. I left it all behind on the bank of the Mississippi."

Maggie blushed and slapped him lightly on the arm. "Oscar!"

"I wish you'd written more often," he whispered. "I only got five letters from you. I wrote to you whenever I could."

"I wrote to you every day. I only got three of your letters."

"Next to the dysentery, not getting your letters was the worst part of the war."

"But you're home. Have you heard from Uncle Stub?"

"No. He's in the 123rd New York Volunteers. They were somewhere in Virginia I think. That was the last we heard from him. We don't know where he is now."

"He'll come home. We won at Vicksburg and Gettysburg. The war's almost over."

"God willing."

"And what will you do now, Oscar? What happens now that you're home?"

"I'll start back with Van Kleeck's in a few days making brushes. He's building a small brush-making factory in Waterford on the river bank, not far from your house. I might see you every day once I start working there instead of in my house."

"That will be nice. I'll look forward to that day."

"Nothing could be better than seeing you every day," Oscar said. He looked around at the others in the park. No one was watching them. He leaned over and gave her a kiss. "Life on the banks of the Hudson is much more pleasant than life on the Mississippi."

Maggie looked down modestly after the kiss. There it was! Among the blades of grass she saw a four-leaf clover. Oscar saw it too and reached across her body to pick it. "For you my lady," he said. "A four-leaf clover. A sign of good luck."

Maggie laughed and took it. "Our good luck should last forever. I'll keep this somewhere safe and everything will always be good for us." She tucked the clover carefully into her purse.

June 1865

"Uncle Stub's home!" Oscar grinned as he said it and couldn't help but hug Maggie even though they stood right there on her front porch where anyone could see them. He had jogged to her house right after work and leaped up the steps to where she waited for him. It had become a daily event, his stopping at her house on his way home from the new wood-walled brush factory the Van Kleeck's had built in Waterford. Today's visit was special with his news about Stub.

"That's wonderful! He's all right? He wasn't wounded?" Maggie shared his excitement but tempered it with her newfound concerns. She had seen what the war did to the other soldiers who survived to return home. She knew the changes in Oscar.

"I think he's all right. I haven't really seen him yet. He got to the house late last night and went right to bed. We're going to have a party tomorrow to welcome him. I expect he's been sleeping all day today. That's what I did most of the day after I got home. Could you come with me tomorrow? It's the weekend, and I won't be at work. Addie and Rollo will be there too."

"Of course. Oh, we do have fun when we get together with Addie and Rollo. And they're getting married soon."

"September. But that can wait. This is Stub's time. Come with me tomorrow and meet Stub."

"I will. Tell me again about your Uncle Stub. What's he like?"

"Sylvester. We call him Stub. He's six years older than Addie and me. And he's more like my big brother than my uncle. He was always looking for excitement, adventures, when we were boys. He would drag me along with him when I was little. I remember this one time. We were down at the river, and he caught two frogs. He gave me one, and he kept the other. We carried them up onto the grass back from the river. Then we had a race, with our two frogs hopping, trying to get back to the river while we chased them, cheering. He's like that. He climbed trees higher than I could imagine. He was fast, a good runner, great at games. I always looked up to Stub."

"You told me they call him Stub because he's short?"

"Yes. I'm not big, but now that we're both grown, I'm a little taller than he is. He's short but strong, and he's a real leader, a natural. People follow him. He's handsome, with curly blond hair. Girls like him. He's got a girlfriend from before the war. Ann McIntyre. I hope she comes tomorrow. She lives with her family out on a farm up in Argyle."

"I expect she'll be there. We all wait for our men to come home from the war. I was there for you. Addie waited for Rollo. How long was Stub gone?"

"He enlisted more than three years ago, right at the start of the war. He was eager to go. It was going to be his next big adventure. So he's been in for the whole war. Even though they signed the treaty in Virginia back in April, it's taken till now for him to get home."

Maggie remembered the big parade and the men returning from the Second Regiment. They were at war for only two years and returned with that haunted look in their eyes. She looked at Oscar, noticing again how thin he had become, and she remembered how quiet he was when he first came home after less than a year. Now Stub was back after so much longer. She dreaded the ways he might have changed from the exciting young man Oscar described for her.

"So you'll come tomorrow?" Oscar asked again. "I can stop by to walk you to my house if you'd like me to."

"Of course."

The next day Oscar and Maggie walked together across the bridge from Waterford to his house. They brought an apple pie she had baked to share at the celebration. It was in a basket, draped with a red checked cotton cloth to keep the flies away. When they arrived, they saw that a small crowd had gathered in the front yard on chairs in the shade. Stub's sister Addie and her friend Rollo sat with Oscar's family. The McIntyres, Stub's girlfriend's family, were also a part of the group.

Stub was not among them. "Where's Stub?" asked Oscar.

Addie answered. "I think he's out back with Ann."

Oscar led Maggie past the lilacs, around the house into the backyard. Stub squatted on the ground next to a small smoky fire. Ann stood nearby under an elm tree, arms crossed, not smiling.

"Hey Stub!" called Oscar. "Welcome home!" They had seen each other briefly around the house before the party but this was his official welcome.

Stub looked up, grinned, and stood, wiping dirt and ashes off his hands on his handkerchief. "Oscar! It's good you could be here today." He hugged Oscar and looked at Maggie. "And who might this be?"

"This is my friend Maggie. I've told her all about you."

"Yes. It's a pleasure to meet you, Miss Maggie. Addie's told me about you as well."

"It's nice to meet you too," Maggie said. "What's with the fire?'

"I'm burning my uniform." Stub shook his head, his brow furrowed. His eyes shifted to the fire. He took a stick and stirred the smoking pile of dark clothes to make the flames flare.

Ann explained, "He said the uniform was full of bugs and this is the best way to get rid of the bugs."

"It's the best way to get rid of the uniform too. I want nothing more to do with it." He kicked at the small fire.

"Come on Stub," said Ann. "Let it burn. Let's go join your family out front."

Stub gave the fire a final poke with the stick and allowed Ann to lead him around the house to the front. Oscar and Maggie followed.

After lunch Rollo and Oscar walked to the backyard of the house with Stub. The women busied themselves gathering the dishes from lunch for washing.

"What can you tell us about the war?" Oscar asked.

"I don't know. You and Rollo were both in the war. You know what it was like." Stub's answer was evasive, an attempt to end the talk. A sudden flash of fear crossed his face and was gone.

But Rollo continued the conversation. "I served in Virginia but only for a few months. We stayed in camp and I didn't really get in any big skirmishes. And Oscar was on the Mississippi. Where were you? Did you see any battles?"

Stub looked up, through the trees, trying to catch the breeze, the cool air blowing up from the Hudson. He said nothing.

Ann overheard the men as she walked past, bringing chairs onto the back lawn. She spoke for him. "Yes, he was in a lot of battles. He doesn't like to talk about it."

Ann went back to the house for more chairs. The men stood quietly. Stub was a friend and an uncle. They didn't want to push the matter.

Stub was silent, leaning forward, staring at the ground between his feet. His hands clenched. He couldn't look at Oscar or Rollo. The memories stormed at him.

No! I wish I could talk about it. I wish I could tell you what happened. But I can't. I wish I could forget. I wish for a lot of things. I was everywhere. The New York 123rd Infantry was in every battle you've heard about. We were in Virginia in the early part of the war. A lot of little skirmishes fighting over crossroads. And we were at Fredericksburg and Chancellorsville, the Wilderness. We were in the middle of it all at Gettysburg, and we chased Lee back to Virginia after that. Then they sent us down to Alabama and we picked up with Sherman, through Georgia. Kennesaw Mountain and Peachtree Creek. The siege of Atlanta. I watched Atlanta burn to the ground. The smell of smoke haunts me. Even that little fire burning my uniform. Later we moved into the Carolinas, burning everything we saw. At the end we came back up through Virginia, fighting all the way. They tell you that the war ended at Appomattox on April 9, but there was still fighting after that. The rebels didn't all take easily to the surrender. Finally, there was the Grand Review of the Armies in Washington a few weeks ago, a big parade, like that's what war is. I was there. And I was mustered out June 8. So, yes, I saw some battles.

Nobody said anything. They waited to hear what Stub would tell them. He took a deep breath but still said nothing.

I know they mean well. They're curious. But they make me think about it. I have the dreams at night, but I try not to think about it during the day when I have some control over my brain.

Oscar and Rollo watched him carefully. Stub looked like he was in a daze, his eyes unfocused. He shook his head like he was trying to scare away gnats. He began to say something, but he stopped. He looked at Oscar and Rollo.

They were good men and good friends, and they'd been in the war too. But he didn't want to share his memories—even with these two fellow soldiers. Still, the memories were there. He couldn't make them go away.

The worst moment for me might have been at Chancellorsville. We'd been camped out near this big mansion back across the river from Fredericksburg, and they called us to help with the attack on a little hill nearby, out from Chancellorsville. We came along early that morning, but the fighting had been going on all the day before, our men trying to take that hill. The rebels were dug in half way up the slope down in a trench, and they had artillery on top.

So I'm with our line, marching toward the hill. Our flag is out front flapping, and drums are beating behind us, and artillery shells are screaming overhead, crashing down around me. Smoke is everywhere. And the rebels behind that trench wall are shooting straight into my line. As I get closer, I'm stepping over bodies. Lots of dead and wounded lying there left from the earlier assaults, the wounded men screaming in pain, dying. The dirt down in Virginia is a rust color, and I see what I thought was thick, red mud. It took a moment for me to understand that it wasn't red dirt. It was red with blood, pools of blood. I'm marching straight at the rebel guns through all that blood.

Oscar and Rollo shifted their feet, uncomfortable with Stub's silence. But they saw his tension. Yes, they all knew. They'd all been in the war. It was hard for all of them, but Oscar and Rollo sensed that what Stub was remembering was far worse than what they had seen.

Maggie, Ann, and Addie came out from the house and rejoined the men, bringing a tray with six sweating glasses of cool lemonade. They pulled the straight-backed chairs into a circle on the grass and eased back in the shade with the lemonade. Embers of tattered cloth still smoldered nearby.

The group sat silently and Maggie saw how Stub was, his face tight, lines around his thin-lipped mouth, his eyes almost filling with tears, focused on the ground. It was the same look she had seen when the Second Regiment returned. Maggie sat with her hands at her mouth, fighting back her own tears. The horror of the war had touched so many men. Now it had claimed Oscar's uncle.

Stub spoke finally, just a few words explaining some of what he had been thinking in silence, hoping that by putting it out there for his friends he could bring an end to the talk of the war. "Chancellorsville and Gettysburg were the same kind of hell. I was never shot. It was like God almighty had his hand on me, protecting me. Men were killed right next to me but I kept on advancing and never got hit. And they kept promoting me every time someone of a higher rank got killed. I was a sergeant when it was all over."

More silence from the now somber group. After some time, Maggie spoke up cheerily, trying to recall her lost ideals, her innocence from before the war, trying to lift the spirits of her friends. "So you're a hero. You weren't wounded, and you came home a hero."

Stub gave a terse laugh. "Oh, I'm no hero. I'm just a survivor."

Ann leaned closer to him and took his hand.

"What will you do now?" asked Addie.

"I don't know. Ann's father talked to me this morning. He asked me if I'd like to help out at his orchard up north in Argyle. I think I might give that a try. I have no need for the crowds here in Lansingburgh. It bothers me to be in the city with all the noise and the horses, and the bustle. The orchard sounds very good. Quiet. Peaceful." Ann continued holding his hand, stroking the back across the tense tendons and veins.

Oscar spoke. "You'll still be around then. Ann's farm isn't that far away." He didn't want to lose touch with Stub now that he was finally home. "We'll still see you when you come into Lansingburgh. And I'll come out to visit you in Argyle."

"Yes, I'll still be around. It's only a few miles north of here. If you come out to the orchard, bring your friend Maggie with you. And maybe Addie and Rollo too. I would enjoy that. I just don't want anything to do with the war anymore. I've already burned my uniform. I brought a few souvenirs home from the war. Now I don't even want them. I'll probably just burn them too."

"What do you have?" Oscar asked.

"I collected confederate money for a while. I took it out of the pockets of the men I'd killed. It seemed like a good idea, the right thing to do in the moments after a battle ended. There's the money and a few other things I brought home with me. Do you want any of it?"

Oscar thought about it. He didn't really want money taken from the pockets of dead men, men his uncle had killed. "No, that's all right," he said.

But Maggie had always been a collector. "I'll take it," she said. "You brought it all the way home. It would be a shame to throw it away."

Stub reached into the dark leather military satchel he still carried with him. He pulled out a packet of paper wrapped in gold foil, tied with twine. "Here," he said. "The money's worthless anyway. It's nothing more than paper now that the war's over. And I'm just as happy to be rid of it."

Maggie tucked the bundle of money into her handbag. "Thank you," she said. "It's gone now. The war's over. You're safe. You're home."

Family Folktales
and Fibs

WHY DO FAMILY STORIES change? Isn't the truth good enough? Sure, there are things we all wish might have been different and stories we would rather erase from our family history. But why rewrite family lore when the facts are what they are?

When I was twelve my English teacher assigned my class one of James Fenimore Cooper's Leatherstocking books, *The Last of the Mohicans.* I enjoyed it and mentioned to my mother that we were reading it in English class.

"Oh, that's wonderful," she said. "You know of course that you're related to the author?"

I was puzzled but intrigued. "Really? How?"

"Your grandmother, my mother, was Grace Cooper. She married James MacMurray, your grandfather. But my mother is a Cooper just like James Fenimore Cooper. We're related."

"Really? That's cool." I went to class the next day and bragged to my teacher and the whole class that my grandmother was related to the author. I was very proud. When we finished *The Last of the Mohicans* my class moved on to studying another book and another author. But I wasn't done. I went to the school library and hunted down other books by James Fenimore Cooper. I read *The Deerslayer,* neglecting the books I was supposed to be reading for

English class. Then I moved on to *The Pathfinder*. All three seemed to be the same story, and I became bored. I noticed there were other books by Cooper in the library, but I had done my duty to my relative by reading three of the Leatherstocking series. Enough was enough.

Decades later, married and with two children, Debbie and I took our kids on a family vacation in upstate New York. One day we went to Cooperstown to see the Baseball Hall of Fame. At the end of the day we left the crowds of tourists, the Hall of Fame, the t-shirt shops and baseball memorabilia and drove out of Cooperstown into the countryside and woodlands. We passed the historic James Fenimore Cooper Art Museum, Homestead and Farm a few miles outside of town. It was late and we wanted to get our kids to dinner and back to the motel. We drove on.

A quick review of the brochures we had picked up in Cooperstown informed me that Cooperstown was settled by James Fenimore Cooper's father. George Washington slept there. The Leatherstocking tales were set on nearby Lake Otsego, Glimmerglass in James Fenimore Cooper's stories. Cooper wrote two lesser known stories about Cooperstown, *The Pioneers* and *Home as Found*. *The Pioneers* was an idyllic frontier-town story that the Cooperstown residents loved. *Home as Found* was a more cynical, satirical book that showed some of the personal issues that arise in small towns. The citizens of Cooperstown preferred *The Pioneers*.

When I returned home from my vacation I checked in with my mother. "Guess where we went on our vacation, Mom?"

"Oh, I don't know. Where?"

"Cooperstown, New York. We went to the Baseball Hall of Fame."

"Oh that's nice." Mom was a casual Red Sox fan. She liked baseball but wasn't passionate about the game.

"Yes, it was great. My kids loved it."

"Good. I'm glad they enjoyed it."

"Yes. But we didn't get to the James Fenimore Cooper Homestead and Farm. We ran out of time. I know it's a part of our heritage but there just wasn't enough time."

"What do you mean it's a part of our heritage?"

"You know, Mom. We're related to James Fenimore Cooper."

"Whatever gave you that crazy idea?"

"You did. You told me we're related to him when I was reading *The Last of the Mohicans* in Junior High."

"Oh, that's ridiculous. I never said such a thing. Why would I tell you we're related to James Fenimore Cooper?"

"I don't know, but you did Mom," I insisted again. "You told me that your mother was related to him. That's why I read all those Leatherstocking tales. Even the ones that weren't assigned."

"I never told you that. I don't know where you got such an idea. It's not true."

I changed the subject. Better to talk about anything rather than debate whether another story she had told me wasn't true.

As the years passed, I began to realize that many of my mother's stories weren't true. Whether it was her account of Oscar and Maggie's life or my supposed relationship to James Fenimore Cooper, my mother made up stories. Of course I'm also a storyteller. I'm making up my imagined chronicle of the lives of Oscar and Maggie to fill the void left by my mother's fabrications about them. It's ironic I suppose. Am I any better with my make-believe world of Oscar and Maggie than my mother with all of her misinformation?

There were also family secrets. In some cases, the secrets were obscured by the fabricated stories she told me, like the ones about our Scottish heritage. Some were topics that we simply didn't discuss. These non-stories often dealt with medical issues. I ought to know my family's medical history but I don't. I know that my mother's father, James MacMurray, died of a heart attack. I don't know for sure the cause of other relatives' deaths. I should.

When my father was fighting kidney and liver cancer I began accompanying him and my mother on their visits to the doctor. On one visit near the end, my father turned to me as we approached the medical office building. "There's something you should know about me in case it comes up during our talk with the doctors."

I saw my mother react, turning to him and whispering, "Do you really think we ought to tell Peter? Why, after all these years? He doesn't need to know about that."

"Yes, it's time," my father said. "He's forty years old. It's time he knew." Then he continued, addressing me directly. "I have a glass eye. I had an accident when I was in college. I was building a set for the drama club and my hammer split a nail and a piece of the nail flew into my eye. I've had a glass eye ever since."

I watched my mother shrink down in her seat in the car, embarrassed and distressed that the truth was suddenly out there.

"That's why I never played catch with you when you were a boy," my father continued. "With only one working eye I lack depth perception. I can't catch very well."

We went into the doctor's office in silence, my mother sullen, me trying to make sense of it all. I began recalling moments when my father would stare oddly and lose focus. I remembered times when my mother nudged him and gestured to his eyes, and he would take off his glasses and wipe his eyes. It all started to become clear. His glass eye looked perfectly normal most of the time. But why hadn't they simply told me about the glass eye years earlier?

Later, going through some of the old family papers I had found, I discovered programs saved from his years in the Emory University Drama Club. His involvement with the drama club while he was a student at Emory was not a casual thing. He was a member of the club for all four undergraduate years and continued with the drama club when he attended Emory in grad school. He was president of the club at least one year. He performed in several plays and was the stage manager for many more. His name is listed frequently in the thick stack of playbills he kept.

All of this is notable because my daughter went to college to study theater. She graduated with a degree in Music Theater and worked as a professional stage manager in several theaters for a while after her graduation. Her involvement with theater began after my father was gone, but why didn't my mother share this bit of information? It would have been nice to know that there might be a genetic root for my daughter's passion for the theater and for stage management.

Family stories become an oral history. They become legends, passed along from one generation to the next. They change as they go, embroidered with fantasy and acquiring details about the way we wish things might have been. Debbie's father Merlin recounts all sorts of stories, not just about his time in the Navy but about his childhood, growing up on the farm in South Dakota, and many more incidents in his life. Some of these are related in this book as a contrast to my mother's fables about the MacMurrays. Merlin's stories also stretch the truth at times, but they remain rooted in real events.

My father occasionally told stories about his Uncle Miles. Uncle Miles had led an adventurous, romantic life. He was a spy in Europe during World War One. He barnstormed as a semi-pro baseball player in the South and Midwest after the war. He might have become a pilot in the early days of aviation. He was a "revenuer" in the Smoky Mountains during Prohibition. My father wasn't sure what might have happened to Uncle Miles. I never met him.

Even the early McMurray family had a story they tried to hush. Oscar had an Uncle Albert, his father James' oldest sibling. Old family genealogies and records are incomplete and inaccurate. There are gaps and mistakes so we only have a few traces of Albert's life. Uncle Albert might have been born in 1825, six years after James, though he could have been born a year or two earlier. He left Lansingburgh abruptly in his teens in 1840. A girlfriend left with him, and they got married suddenly and had a child. When his mother died in 1853, Uncle Albert returned to collect his inheritance. His wife and child weren't with him. He may have gotten divorced shortly after he got married. That alone would have been a disgrace to the McMurray family.

While he was back in Lansingburgh, Albert convinced his sister Charlotte, who was close to his age, to pool her inheritance with his so they could buy a nearby farm together. They bought the farm in his name since women at that time couldn't own property. A few months later, Albert vanished again. He had sold the farm and kept all the money. Charlotte's inheritance was gone. She moved in with her sister Addie, living with Oscar and his parents. Oscar's father James was the stable patriarch of the family.

Albert returned briefly at the start of the Civil War, enlisted, and left again. He never returned. Some records show that he lived until the early twentieth century in San Diego. It's possible that he wasn't killed in the civil war. Did he run off to the west or somewhere else during or after the war? Are there other children of Albert's lineage roaming around that we don't know about? My mother fretted often about genealogists finding a horse thief. That would be our Uncle Albert.

My mother told a beautiful story every Christmas. She had an antique Christmas tree ornament, a blown glass bunch of grapes painted gold with a twisted brass stem embedded as a hook. The grapes were kept cushioned with cotton balls in a cardboard box. The story about the grapes was typed on an old piece of paper, brittle where it was folded. It is the only family story we preserved on paper rather than just by recitation, an oral history.

My mother would relate the story as she took the glass grapes from the box each Christmas, cradling the ornament in her hands like a religious relic. One of our ancestors on my grandmother's side, Fieldings not Coopers, brought the grapes with them when they sailed to America from England. The mother of this immigrant family died shortly before they came. The father and his two boys traveled, bringing the grapes as a cherished memory of their mother. Hanging it on their tree each year kept her with them at Christmas in their new home in America. When my mother passed away, my sister got the grapes. They now hang year-round from a stand on a table in her home in France.

There are also stories from Debbie's mother's side; stories about Swedes immigrating to America and Germans working on pineapple or sugar plantations in Hawaii. Many of Debbie's family tales are romantic love stories. Some of them might be true. Christmas traditions abound with Debbie's

Swedish upbringing. Saint Lucia with her crown of evergreen and candles is featured and there are Swedish ornaments. Special holiday treats are served each year at Christmas; herring and several varieties of cookies and baked deserts. Swedish folktales about seasonal farm elves called Tomtens and about other fairy creatures are parts of Debbie's Christmas heritage.

Another Swedish story that Debbie learned from her grandmother Erma Dahlquist is about the small travelling spinning wheel we have sitting in our front hall. According to Erma, the spinning wheel was a wedding gift to Erma's grandmother Olivia when she married Anders Olaf Dahlquist. In Erma's story, Olivia was a lady-in-waiting to the Princess of Sweden but Anders was a simple tailor, a man from beneath Olivia's social class. Because of this class difference, the young lovers were shunned when they married. Olivia was disowned by her parents, and her name was stricken from the Royal Court registry. But the Princess cared about Olivia, understood her love for Anders, and gave Olivia and Anders the spinning wheel as a wedding gift. After the wedding, with no future where they were, Olivia and Anders left Sweden, sailed around the horn, and settled with Anders' brother in a Swedish community in Longview, Washington. The spinning wheel has been passed down to the oldest Dahlquist descendant daughter ever since.

Several years ago, through the miracle of the internet, Debbie established contact with relatives back in Sweden. While touring Scandinavia we added a few days to go meet her family on the Swedish island of Gotland in the middle of the Baltic Sea. We stayed in an ancient hotel in Visby, a walled medieval town on the west coast of Gotland.

On our second day in Gotland we left Visby and drove south to the village of Grotlingbo. We followed directions given by her relative Lars Goransson and found the family farm. Debbie's family has lived in and around Grotlingbo for many generations. We sat in the farmhouse kitchen drinking coffee and becoming acquainted with Lars, his wife Helene and his daughter Olivia. Debbie's ancestors had built this farmhouse centuries ago. When Lars took us to the medieval stone church a kilometer up the road we found the marriage record for Anders and Olivia and saw gravestones of other relatives.

That evening, after a dinner of pancakes with lingonberries, chocolate cake with raspberries and more coffee, Debbie told the story of Olivia and our spinning wheel. Lars burst out laughing. He bounded up the stairs to the attic of the farmhouse and brought down an old wooden cradle made of wood that matched our spinning wheel. The cradle, Lars said had been in his family for generations as well. It too had a family story behind it. But the story he told of Olivia and Anders was different and less romantic than ours.

According to Lars, Olivia and Anders grew up on neighboring farms in Grotlingbo. No princess was involved. Anders and his brother left their farms in a lean year and came to New York. They stayed a year, made some money and returned to Gotland to collect their families. Lars' story about their return to America is the same as Debbie's. Olivia and Anders sailed around the horn and settled in Longview with Anders brother's family. Lars showed us detailed charts he had made tracing the family histories.

So what about the romantic story of the young lovers in the court of Sweden, shunned by their families and running to America? Current speculation is that Olivia told this fabrication to her children and grandchildren after Anders had died. That's how Debbie's grandmother Erma came to know about the spinning wheel and the Princess of Sweden.

Debbie and her family now laugh about the two versions of the spinning wheel story. We prefer the story with the two shunned lovers even though we know it's not true.

What does all of this have to do with Oscar and Maggie? The family-approved story about my great-grandparents is vague, incomplete, filled with inaccuracies and outright lies. The most obvious is the bit about my Irish or Scottish heritage. There are so many other odd instances where the family stories about Oscar and Maggie have turned out to be fabrications. My mother never laughed about the inconsistencies in her stories. There are family secrets, horse thieves, and other shameful things in our past. There are secrets that must be kept. There is nothing funny about hiding truths we would rather forget. It is serious business. I continue my investigation of their lives now doubting everything.

14

Christmas, 1865

OSCAR SAT NEXT TO Maggie on the red sofa in her parlor. He felt cramped, pressed between the rolled red horsehair of the sofa arm, the stuffed pillows, and Maggie. Her parents sat across from them in wingback arm chairs next to the Christmas tree. The tree was short but thick, decorated with glass balls. Tiny candles, securely fastened to branches, were carefully set low enough to keep their small flames clear of the branches above. A fire in the fireplace warmed the room. Oscar felt awkward and out of place amid the cushions and the decorations. His house was crowded with people but lacked the lavish furnishings of Maggie's house. He had become accustomed to Maggie's home and her parents, but this Christmas day was different. He had plans that would make the day special.

"I've got a Christmas present for you," said Oscar. He handed Maggie a thick package wrapped in plain white paper, tied with a thin green ribbon.

"Why Oscar, thank you." Moments earlier, she had given him a gift basket filled with cookies she had baked.

Maggie untied the ribbon and gently pulled the paper open where Oscar had sealed it with gum. She put the paper aside and looked at the book. *The Flowers Personified.* She admired the cover and traced her fingertips over the dark leather, the gold lettering and decorative trim. "Oh, Oscar, it's lovely!" Maggie leaned to him and gave his arm a squeeze.

He sat back smiling waiting for her to open the book. She did and found the inscription in his careful, flowing handwriting on the flyleaf inside the front cover.

Miss Maggie J. Teachout
From her Friend
Oscar E. McMurray
Christmas 1865.

Maggie read the words silently, smiled, and leaned over again, kissing his cheek, not caring that they were right there in front of her parents.

"This is so beautiful," she said as she began turning the pages, admiring the delicate engravings and the hand-tinted pastel colors, pictures of maidens and flowers. She read aloud a short passage from the introduction.

> *Will you never, ladies, take pity on those poor flowers, which are the most frequent tribute laid at your feet? Will you not remember that they are severed from their parent stems: that they have been brought to you that you may see them die, and inhale their last fragrant sighs?*
>
> *I once knew two lovers, who were severed by a cruel destiny. At the close of a long separation they died, without again seeing one another. They were not permitted to correspond, - but to one of them an ingenious device occurred. Without exciting suspicion, they sent to each other the seeds of the flowers which they mutually cultivated. They thus knew, though two hundred leagues apart, that they had the same objects of interest. At the same season of the year, and on the same day, they saw the same flowers expand, and they inhaled the same odors. This was a pleasure – and it was their only pleasure. – Alphonse Karr*

Maggie blushed, sensing a deeper message in Oscar's gift to her. She remembered the months he had been away at war and how she had worried every moment about his safety. She knew that he too had suffered through that separation. She closed the book and sat with it in her lap, her palms resting on the cover. "It's wonderful Oscar. Wherever did you find it?"

"It's a new book, published in New York City. I found it in a book shop in Albany while I was there on business for Mr. Van Kleeck. I like books and stop there often when I get down to Albany. I thought of you as soon as I saw it and told the shop owner to hold a copy aside for me. I saved my money and made a special trip back a few weeks ago to buy it."

Maggie opened the book again, turning the pages carefully, looking at the water-colored engravings. "I see that it was originally written in France, and it's been translated. Very nice. Very elegant and fashionable. I can't wait to read it. Oh Oscar, I will treasure this forever." She closed the book again and clasped it to her chest.

Maggie's father stood and took his wife's hand. "Come along," he said. "Let's go see how dinner is coming in the kitchen." He led her out of the room and tactfully left Oscar with their daughter in the parlor. As soon as they were gone, Oscar and Maggie kissed again.

After dinner, Oscar approached Mr. Teachout, taking his elbow and leading him to a quiet corner of the dining room. "Sir, might I have a word in private?"

"Certainly." Maggie's father believed he knew what was coming. This young man had been courting his daughter for a long time. He led Oscar out to the cold air on the porch where they could be alone, leaving the women in the kitchen.

Oscar began the speech he had silently rehearsed for weeks. "Mr. Teachout, I think the world of your daughter. We have known each other for several years now, and we have become the best of friends. I can't imagine a life without her. I have a good job with the Van Kleeck's. I make a good income. I can provide for her. I would like to ask your permission to ask her for her hand in marriage."

Oscar stood back and looked anxiously at Mr. Teachout. He waited. Mr. Teachout stroked his beard for a moment, tormenting Oscar with his delayed answer. Then he smiled. "Of course. You may ask her. I expect she will say yes. Of course I give my consent for you to marry her. What took you so long?"

"Well, there was the war and everything. I've wanted to come to you about this for a long time, but it never seemed to be the right time. Thank you, sir. I am very pleased that you give me your consent."

"Not at all. You have my blessing. Let's keep this between just the two of us until you've asked her and she's agreed. But I'm very pleased that you want to take this step. Now let's get back inside where it's warm."

Mr. Teachout clapped Oscar on his shoulder. He wrapped his arm around the young man and they went back inside the house, into the warmth and the cinnamon scents of the kitchen. Maggie was at the kitchen table with her mother, busy preparing biscuits for the oven. She missed it when her father caught her mother's eye, smiled, winked, and nodded. Mother smiled in return and gave Maggie a quiet hug.

*****

That evening, as he was about to leave for the frigid walk back through the dark across the bridge to Lansingburgh, Oscar stood on the porch with

Maggie. They kissed quickly.

"I'll see you tomorrow after work," Maggie said. She hugged herself against the cold, eager to get back inside her house.

"Wait a minute," said Oscar. "I have to ask you something." He set her gift basket of cookies aside.

"All right, but hurry. It's freezing out here." She shivered.

"Would you marry me?" He had a longer speech prepared and memorized, just like the speech he had recited to her father. But in the moment, this was all he could muster.

Maggie stopped. She looked at Oscar. She beamed and kissed him again. "Of course, you silly boy! Of course! Did you even doubt that I would say yes?"

Then she paused, no longer feeling the chill. "Have you discussed this with my father?"

"Yes. Earlier this evening. He gave his consent."

Maggie exulted in the moment, hugging Oscar, aroused as much by the proposition alone as by her love for this man who was now planning to live with her forever. Then she pulled back, thoughtful.

"Where would we live?" she asked.

"I don't know. There's not enough room at my house for both of us, even now that Addie and Rollo are married and she's moved off with him. There are still my brother and my sisters and my parents and Aunt Sarah. I can't afford a place of my own. Our own. Not yet. But I will. We can figure that out in time. The important thing is that we've agreed to do this."

Maggie threw her arms around his neck and kissed him again. They were alone on her porch, the biting cold keeping her neighbors inside their houses. "I love you Oscar McMurray."

"I love you too Maggie Teachout. Now get back inside and stay warm. I've got to get home and tell my family about all this."

They hugged, then parted, their hands tracing down each other's arms till just their fingertips touched.

"I'll see you after work," Oscar called as he leaped down her steps, jumped her gate, and began jogging back to Lansingburgh carrying her basket of cookies.

Maggie rushed back into the warmth of her house. She was flushed. Her parents sat in their accustomed chairs in the parlor. Looking down shyly she stood before them and announced, "Oscar just asked to marry me. I said yes."

Without another word, allowing no discussion with her parents, she took her new book and hurried up the stairs to her bedroom. She opened the small drawer in the table by her bed where she had kept Oscar's picture during his time away at the war. The picture was still there though she had less need to look at it every day and kiss it goodnight now that Oscar himself was home and with her. Beneath the picture she found the four-leaf clover they had picked in the park on the riverbank the day he came home. She opened the book, laid the clover carefully between the pages, and closed the book. Finally, she prepared for bed and kissed Oscar's picture once more, like when he was away at war. Once more for luck. She lay for hours, smiling, dreaming, but unable to sleep.

15

Cruising on the
USS Slater

"HI SWEETHEART!" MERLIN'S VOICE boomed out of Debbie's cell phone. I could hear it across the room.

"Hi Daddy. What's up?"

"I wanted to ask you a question. You know I keep in touch with the boys who served on the *USS Spangler*, right?" His deep voice resonated throughout the room.

"Yes," Debbie answered.

From across the room I shouted, "I thought that when you were in the Navy you played football for the base teams in San Diego and Pearl Harbor."

"Hi, Pete," Merlin called out. Debbie put him on speaker phone. "Yes, I played quarterback for our teams. But that's another story or two. This is about my time on the *Spangler*, the ship I served on. We went out to sea all the time."

"So," Debbie continued. "You've been in touch with the *Spangler* crew. What's up?"

"We're planning another reunion on a weekend in May. There's a sister ship to the *Spangler* that's docked like a museum in Albany, New York. The *USS Slater*. It's a Buckley class DE766 just like the *Spangler*. All our *Spangler* veterans are planning to meet there and tour the *Slater*. How far is Albany from Providence? Do you want to meet me in Albany for the weekend?"

"It's about three hours away. Maybe a little more."

Debbie looked at me for agreement. I nodded. "Sure," she said. "Let us know the date and we'll be there."

We left after work on a Friday, stopped briefly for dinner, and arrived around nine o'clock at the hotel where the *Spangler* boys were staying. As we were checking into the hotel, loud voices and laughter came from the bar. We looked in and saw one corner of the room filled with old gentlemen, most wearing Navy baseball caps labeled *USS Spangler*. Merlin sat at a table in the middle of the noise. He saw us and called us over for introductions.

"This is my daughter Debbie, and this is my son-in-law Peter. And these are the boys," he said, his wide hands cupped as he swept out his arms to show off the crew.

The boys were old. All had gray or white hair, thinning or gone in some cases. One used a walker. All were grinning, and some appeared to be well along on the beer. They shouted greetings to us and asked if we wanted to join them for a drink. Debbie got a glass of white wine. I ordered a beer.

"You drink beer?" joked one of the old sailors. "Merlin doesn't drink anything but Coke."

Merlin smiled and explained in his John Wayne voice, "Beer tastes like horse piss. Can't even smell the stuff let alone drink it."

I turned to him. "How do you know it tastes like horse piss? I mean have you ever, you know... I mean I know you grew up on a farm in South Dakota but..."

Merlin sat back with an abashed smile and took a sip of his Coke.

Debbie and I sat with the men for a while, listening to their sailor stories. Then we excused ourselves to go to bed. It had been a long week and a long Friday evening drive. We were tired. Merlin and his shipmates stayed behind swapping stories in the bar.

The next morning after breakfast the sailors began gathering in a hotel meeting room. The plan was for them to spend the morning reliving their Navy days, have a buffet lunch, and then head down to the river to tour the *Slater*.

The *Spangler* had been decommissioned more than a decade earlier and had been scuttled. One enterprising *Spangler* vet had salvaged key mementos before all was lost. An officers' mess tablecloth with a Navy emblem and the embroidered name *USS Spangler* now hung on the wall of the banquet room like a banner. Table settings, flatware, and other *Spangler* memorabilia were spread on a table. Everyone examined the loot and commented, remembering incidents that each item dredged up.

The *USS Slater*, the ship now in Albany, had almost suffered a similar fate. But when it was ready to be decommissioned, the U.S. government sold it to Greece. It had served the Greek Navy for more than a decade before they wore it out. Now it was tied to a dock in Albany as a naval museum. Both the *Spangler* and the *Slater* were destroyer escorts, small, fast mini-warships.

A dozen old sailors sat at tables near the food buffet in the hotel meeting room. They had all served on the *Spangler* at different times. Only a few had seen actual combat at the end of World War II. Most had never met until they discovered the *Spangler* veterans online. But they all shared the common bond of having lived a few formative years of their lives on the same ship. Since their Navy days, their lives had taken different turns. Some had prospered, others had not. One was a wealthy cattle rancher, now from Wyoming, still riding out every day on his horse to check on his herd even though he was in his eighties. Most were retired from a variety of businesses. They were all older, but most were in remarkably good health.

With the sailors on one side of the room, Debbie and I joined the camp followers at tables on the other side. Sitting next to me was a man possibly forty years old. He indicated the elderly vet who used the walker and quietly confided, "That's my dad. Bob. He has cancer and isn't expected to last six more months. This is his last great adventure. He asked me to drive him to Albany from Indiana to be with his shipmates one last time."

Most of the others at our table were Navy wives. We listened with tolerance from across the room as the tall tales about their Navy days got louder and more unbelievable.

"So we walked into that bar in San Diego, and I saw my shipmate sitting there at a table with a bunch of the other guys. And he called to me, 'Mitch I thought you were covering my duty tonight?' And I yelled back, 'I thought we agreed you were going to cover mine!'"

The old sailors roared, slapping each other's backs.

"We'd been at sea for almost a week when we realized that we had loaded on a double order of bacon and an awful lot of beans. But we hadn't got enough eggs to last the rest of our time out at sea. Boy, the breakfasts got interesting that last week we were out!"

More laughter filled the room.

I took a sip of coffee and turned to a white-haired woman sitting at the table with Debbie and me. I asked the woman, "Who are you here with? Which one is yours?"

"I'm with Edward," she said, pointing to a tall man with wavy white hair. "He's the one over there with the glasses. He was a lieutenant when he was on the *Spangler*. Sometimes he was at the helm when they were sailing."

"Tell me about Edward. How did you meet him? What was he like when he was in the Navy?"

"Edward... Oh, he was something! People always said he looked just like Burt Lancaster back then. You know, the movie star? He was so handsome! Girls used to stop in the street and stare at him when we walked by." The woman's face shone with her excitement as she talked.

"How did you meet him?" I repeated.

"I was going to college back in Boston. I had a boyfriend, but he was pretty boring. I'd always loved to go dancing, but this boy wasn't the kind who liked to dance. So one of my girlfriends and I took one evening a week and we'd go down to the USO. This was during Korea, just a few years after World War Two, and the USO was still a big deal. We'd go down there and meet some of the sailors and laugh and dance. Sometimes my boyfriend would tag along, but he never was much for the dancing. He'd just sit there and watch."

"So what about Edward," I asked again.

She laughed, her eyes glowing with the excitement of her story. "Be patient! I'm getting to him. It took years for me to meet him. You have to wait for me to tell about it."

"Okay," I said. I too laughed and sat back to wait for her to continue.

Her voice took on a conspiratorial tone as she went on with her story. She leaned toward me and almost whispered as though she were sharing a rumor. "So, this one night, I'm there with my girlfriend and my boyfriend. We're sitting there, not dancing, just having a Coke or something. But I had noticed Edward at the bar as soon as we came in. We'd hardly settled in at our table when he came right over and asked me to dance. I looked at my boyfriend, but he just gave me a little wave as though to say, 'Go ahead. You know I don't like dancing. You go have a bit of fun.' So off I went with Edward. And the moment he put his arms around me to dance I was gone. He was the one, I just knew it. We must have danced for hours that night. And at some point I realized that my girlfriend and my old boyfriend had left. Edward walked me home afterwards. And he was waiting for me at my dormitory the next night to take me dancing again."

"That's quite a story," I said, smiling, watching how she brightened as she relived her meeting with Edward.

"There's more!" She laughed again and continued with her story. "My parents weren't at all happy about Edward. They wanted me to marry my old boyfriend because he came from what people called 'a good family'. All they knew about Edward was that he was a sailor. That's all I knew then, too.

But that was enough for me. I was in love with him, and our time together was short. He was getting shipped off to the west coast in about a week."

"What happened when he left?" I asked.

"I cried for days on end," she said. "I went home to my parents and just cried. But I wrote to Edward every day in San Diego. And he wrote to me. And one day his letter came in with a one-way train ticket for me to go out and join him in San Diego. So off I went. My parents just about went crazy. But what else could I do? We had to be together. Do you understand that?"

"Oh yes. Oh, I understand that," I said.

"Do you? Well, there are certain things that are more accepted today than they were back then. But kids in love are still the same, I think. When I ran off to Edward in San Diego? We moved in together out there. Why do you think my parents were so upset? Then he proposed. The first time he came home on leave after being out at sea we got married. A very simple small wedding. Just the two of us and a couple of his buddies from the base at a civil ceremony."

"And now here you are. Still together and visiting Albany, New York."

"That's right. We've been married sixty years now. Children, grandchildren, the whole bit. When you meet the right one, you both know it, and it can't be denied."

The boys on the other side of the room were standing up. They handed maps around explaining how to get down to the river and find the *Slater*. We were off.

We parked near the dock and walked to the ship. As the veterans climbed the gangplank, each stopped for a moment at the top and saluted the flag before stepping on board. "We're addressing the colors," Merlin explained. "It's protocol."

The men fanned out on the ship, wandering the gray steel-walled rooms and corridors. The *Slater* had been reserved for the veterans that afternoon so no regular tourists were on board. A Navy sailor was stationed with the ship to handle visitors, but he quietly walked to the dock, stretched a chain across the gang plank and gave the veterans their space. Merlin led Debbie and me up to the radio room and showed us the tiny space where he had worked while on the *Spangler*.

While we were there another old gentleman approached. "What are you folks doing in the radio room?" he asked. "I'm the radio man."

"So was I!" grinned Merlin. "Dit dit, dah dah, dah dah, dit, dit dah dit, dit dah dit dit, dit dit, dah dit."

The other radio man answered. "Dit dit, dah dah, dit dah dah dah, dah dah

dah,dit dit dit dit dit, dah dit!"

They laughed, shook hands, and clapped each other on the shoulders, sharing a message only they understood. Their connection was more than just duty on the *Spangler*.

Then we wandered around the old ship following Merlin. He showed us the bunks, the mess, the bridge, the gun mounts. The other *Spangler* veterans roamed the ship around us.

There was a moment when Bob's son assisted him from his walker into the seat of a big gun on the foredeck. "This was my station when I was on the *Spangler*," Bob said.

He fiddled with the gun and pulled a pin out from the gears beneath it. Then, frail as he was, he began swinging the gun around, tipping it up and down, aiming it at targets on the far bank of the Hudson River. When a long white luxury yacht glided by us on the river, heading toward New York City, Bob lined it up in the gun sight and tracked it. He spoke without taking his eye away from the gun sight. "There's a stack of ammo right there on the deck. Do you think it's live? I could take that big yacht right out if I wanted to."

Edward stood in the middle of the deck, arms crossed, feet spread, surveying the ship and his crew. A crowd of the white-haired veterans gathered around him. "We've got everyone we need," Edward announced. "Mitch, you could go down to your regular post in the engine room and fire her up. Merlin, you and your buddy can take shifts in the radio room. We've even got a cook on board. And Bob there can man the gun if anyone gives us trouble. It's just a thought, but the only things connecting us to shore are two ropes and the gangplank. What do you say boys? Should we cast off and take her out for a cruise?"

Among the veterans, there were grins all around. But there were anxious looks on the faces of the wives, Bob's son, and I'm sure on Debbie's face and mine. The old sailors slowly gave up the fantasy of attacking New York City after running down and sinking the white yacht. An hour later we all went ashore and the Navy curator opened the *Slater* to the public again. New war stories had been born, ready to be expanded, embellished, and perfected as time passed.

Drawing of Ship by Oscar

Swedish Spinning Wheel

Stereoscope

Oscar's Brushes

Richelieu Terrace

Lansingburgh Ann Street House

Young Maggie

Maggie

Sylvester McMurray

Confederate Money

Oscar in uniform

Oscar

A young James H. MacMurray   *James H. MacMurray*

Tin Soldiers

For Baby Edna

Merlin Carr

Uncle Miles; J. Gordon Stipe Jr. on right

Hummerdale

Merlin at 45mm

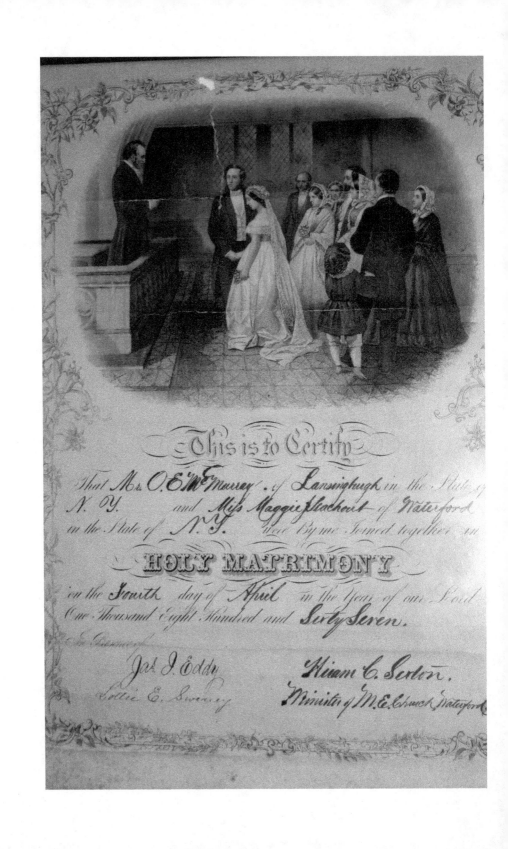

This is to Certify

That Mr. O. E. McMurray of Lansingburgh in the State of N. Y. and Miss Maggie Stachout of Waterford in the State of N. Y. were By me Joined together in

HOLY MATRIMONY

in the Fourth day of April in the Year of our Lord One Thousand Eight Hundred and Sixty Seven.

In Presence of

Jas. J. Eddy

Lottie E. Sweeney

Hiram C. Sexton.

Minister of M. E. Church Waterford

16

The Wedding
April 4, 1867

LIKE SO OFTEN IN April in upstate New York, the wedding day was cool. Light rain fell during the morning. Oscar waited with James, his best friend from their years at Lansingburgh Academy, in a stark white-walled back room of Maggie's Methodist church in Waterford. James was also a brushmaker at Van Kleeck's. He and Oscar walked together most mornings from Lansingburgh across the bridge to the brushmaking factory in Waterford. At the end of their work days James walked home alone while Oscar visited Maggie. Today, James served as best man. He and Oscar had discussed the wedding on many of their morning walks.

Oscar fidgeted, unable to stand for long, but restless whenever he sat. "Wouldn't you know it?" he said. "The biggest day of my life, and it's raining."

James pulled at his white cotton dress gloves, tucking them up between each finger. He straightened his narrow bow tie and checked Oscar's as well. They weren't accustomed to being dressed in this manner, in suits, except on Sunday. He draped his arm across Oscar's shoulder and laughed. "They say that rain on your wedding day is a good omen. Besides, just be happy it isn't snow or sleet."

Pastor Sexton nodded, smoothing his thin hair back across his scalp. He had done this before, taking young men, edgy as untrained colts, calming them as he prepared to lead them to the altar and their brides. "That's right," he assured Oscar. "Everything will be fine. You're nervous but you and Margaret know what you're doing. How long have you known each other?"

The reverend had counseled the young couple during the past few weeks, and he knew the answer to his question. It was nothing more than talk designed to calm the groom.

Oscar paused, counting the years. "We met six years ago. And we began courting then. But there was the war. It just wasn't the right time till now. We became engaged at Christmas a year and a half ago."

"You'll be fine," Pastor Sexton repeated. "Try to relax. It's almost time for us to go in the sanctuary."

They entered the back of the hushed church and stood by the altar. Candles lit the shadowy sanctuary. With the rain, the light through the stained-glass windows was diffused and dim. A small crowd of their friends and relatives, no more than three dozen people, sat in the first few rows of pews, talking quietly. Now the talking ended and everyone looked at Oscar and James and the Pastor. Oscar, ill-at-ease anytime he was in front of a crowd, became more anxious than usual, this being his wedding day, his moment.

Oscar caught the eye of Stub in the second row and grinned. Stub was engaged now to Ann. His turn would come soon. Stub clasped his hands and raised them over his head laughing silently. Oscar was confused as to whether Stub was praying for him or pantomiming the gesture of an athletic champion celebrating a victory. Either way it made Oscar laugh quietly. He relaxed.

The pianist began to play Mendelssohn's "Wedding March" and the congregation stood. Oscar began to sweat. Then he saw Maggie.

She came down the aisle on her father's arm. Her long dress was fashioned with two ruffles of lace, draped down from her neck over her shoulders. The sleeves fell over her wrists almost to her fingers. She had a matching lace veil trimmed with flowers. Bare-handed, she carried a tiny bouquet. Her childhood friend Lottie Sweeney and her mother had spent most of the morning getting Maggie ready, fastening the many clasps on the back of the dress, arranging the flowers and the veil.

Maggie caught Oscar's eyes and smiled. Again he relaxed. In the midst of all the dressed-up attire and the pomp of the ceremony it still came down to just the two of them, right there, together and in love. This was perfect.

Maggie's father kissed her on the cheek, shook Oscar's white-gloved hand and stepped back. Best man James stood next to Oscar; Lottie Sweeney waited at Maggie's side.

The Reverend Sexton began speaking, and moments later Oscar and Maggie were married. There was a small dinner in the hall behind the church; meals prepared by both the McMurray and Teachout families. The mood was jovial. Both families toasted the newlyweds with glasses of cider. Loud conversation, jokes, and laughter dominated the hall, echoing off the white walls. Late in the afternoon the festivities concluded.

The rain had ended and sunlight began to glow with a bright clarity on the wet leaves and new buds on the trees. Oscar's father took the newlyweds aside quickly while they waited for James to bring the carriage. "You can both settle into your regular room. Maggie, I put your things there this morning before coming to church. I'll be taking Sarah back to her family in Columbus, Ohio in a few weeks. Until then, we'll be sharing the house. It will be yours when we leave."

"That's fine, Father. Thank you," Oscar replied, unable to look at his father in this moment where they were speaking so frankly about Maggie moving into the McMurray house. "We'll be fine. And Maggie can help Sarah with the cooking and other chores while you and I are off at work."

James, doing his final duty as best man, pulled the carriage up to the church. As the guests applauded, Oscar and Maggie got in the second seat for the ride back to the house in Lansingburgh. Along the way, acquaintances saw the carriage, clapped, and called out their best wishes. The newlyweds waved back, laughing.

*****

That night, Maggie settled in the narrow bed waiting for Oscar. She reached for her bag and took out *The Flowers Personified*. She opened it to a favorite passage and placed her small wedding bouquet next to the binding between the pages. Carefully she pressed the book closed. The bouquet, like the four-leaf clover she had found on the picnic the day Oscar came home from the war, was preserved forever. She hugged the book quickly and returned it to her bag.

Oscar came into his cramped bedroom, nervous, unable to make eye contact with his new bride. He blew out the lamp and slid into the narrow bed with Maggie. Quietly, sensitive to the small house and the thin walls that separated them from Aunt Sarah in her bedroom next door and from his father in his room down the hall, Oscar and Maggie made love.

*****

The next days were awkward in the crowded house. The newlyweds were in one bedroom. Father was in the master bedroom he had shared with Hannah before her passing. Sarah occupied the tiny third bedroom that had been hers for the years she had stayed in the house with her sister and James.

111

Now, they all led their lives in respectful silence, eating their meals together, bumping into each other as they passed in the halls, and tactfully allowing each other as much space as possible in the small house.

They shared the household duties, the women cooking and doing the cleaning and laundry, the men tending to the yard and splitting firewood when they weren't working at the brushmaking factory across the river in Waterford. It was a congenial house, but Oscar and Maggie privately counted the days till Father would pack Sarah and her belongings and take her on the trip west to Ohio and her family. It was not uncommon for a man to look after his wife's maiden sister but propriety said that an unmarried woman should not be residing in the same house as an unmarried man. Now that Hannah had passed, Sarah should return to her own family.

Work at Van Kleeck's slowed after the war. Father seemed restless. One night after dinner he confided in Oscar, "I'm not a young man, but I believe I am still strong enough for life on the frontier. When I take Sarah out to Ohio I think I'd like to continue on farther west and make a home somewhere in a town on the prairie. I could find work in a shop or hire myself out as a farmhand. I anticipate the brushmaking business will continue to slow in the years ahead. Fashion doesn't demand as many brushes now for so many different purposes. I could leave that business to you and the other young fellows. Would you be all right if I stayed out west?"

Oscar nodded thoughtfully. "Yes, Father. Maggie and I will be fine. We'll miss you though. You've always been here. Except for when I was away in the war, I've always lived in the same house as you."

"You could come with me, son. Your brother and sisters, Eugene, Sarah Emma, and Anna Marie have agreed to accompany us to Ohio. You could start a new life on the prairie as well. With the railroad coming to Troy we've become just another stop along the rail line. The canals are less important and the whole region seems to be declining. You could use a new start too."

"Yes, we've thought of that, but Maggie's family is here. She belongs here in Lansingburgh, near Waterford. We'll stay."

"We'll still be in touch with each other. The mail is more reliable now than it was during the war. We can write to each other."

"We will."

A week later, James and Sarah left for Ohio. Even more than on his wedding day, Oscar felt like a new chapter of his life was beginning. He was alone now with just Maggie, without the support of his father and the companionship of his family. The house was quiet in the evenings. He missed his family but enjoyed the freedom of having only Maggie to come home to after work each day.

Oscar received letters several times a month. In the fall, six months after they left, James' letter brought the startling news that he and Sarah had married in Ohio. A year later, his letter told of their decision to move further west to Minnesota. Except for one brief visit to Ohio, Oscar never saw his father again.

17

Changes
Lansingburgh,
November 1867

MAGGIE'S LAMB STEW WAS finished and Oscar had cleared the dinner table. The small chocolate cake he had bought at the bakery on his way home from Van Kleeck's still sat on the table, missing the two slices he and Maggie had eaten to conclude their six-month anniversary dinner. They now reclined against each other on the hard sofa in the parlor of their house on Ann Street.

Oscar was the first to speak, setting the mood. "Everything moves so fast these days. It's not like back in the old days when life was slow and easy."

Maggie nodded. "What's happened to us? We're always busy, but it's not bad to be living this way. Our life is good right now, isn't it?"

"Yes, of course. Ah, the silence. I do enjoy the peace and quiet here," said Oscar. "It's nice to be alone here in our home. Still, with everything that's happened to us these past few years, sometimes it makes me anxious."

Maggie rested her hand and her cheek on his chest. "Yes. But it's peaceful tonight. This is nice."

Oscar stroked Maggie's arm, reminiscing. "So much has happened since the war, maybe too much. That was the beginning of it all for me, the war and the homecoming."

Maggie nodded. "You've moved on. We've both moved on. Our lives are different now."

"That's true," Oscar agreed. "But after I got home from the war, my house was always crowded with people coming and going. For a while there were nine of us living here. It was always noisy. There was no privacy. Even after Mom died it was still chaotic with all the people living here."

"I know. My house was a bit larger and my family was smaller. You must have enjoyed stopping by to visit me."

"Yes, but not because it was quiet. I was there to see you."

Maggie smiled and hugged him closer. "Yes, I liked that of course. And then we were married."

"But you remember how it was when we were first married. Dad and my Aunt Sarah were here too. I understand that Dad felt obligated to take care of Sarah since she was never married, but it meant that we always had people around. That's why I like it now with just the two of us here."

Maggie nodded. "We had to wait to get married till everyone moved away. There was no room for us to live here."

"It took time," Oscar explained. "The changes have left us here together with this house. But it was hard. Part of it had to do with Mom's passing. When Mom got sick last year with consumption, her passing was so sudden. I understand all too well that death is a part of life. Not just what I saw in the war, but right here. I was nine when the scarlet fever went through my family. I lost two sisters that year. Little Anna was born two years later. And Grandma Spicer died when I was ten. It seems like there was always someone dying, one funeral after another."

Maggie became suddenly solemn, remembering the deaths in her own family. She settled in comforting her husband, hugging him close again. "I know. People died in my family too."

Oscar continued. "Yes. We both know how it is. It happens. After Mom died and we got married, Dad took Sarah back to be with her family out west. Eugene and my two sisters went on to Ohio with Dad and Sarah. Then we got word that Dad and Aunt Sarah were married in Ohio and settled with her family out there. Now I read in Dad's letters that they're thinking they'll move farther west to Michigan or Minnesota. They'll be living out there in some frontier town. I might never see my dad again."

"It must feel empty for you here but now we have the house to ourselves," said Maggie.

"Yes. That's good. But there have been so many changes. Now Stub and Ann are getting married in two months. I'm happy for them, but it's just so much. I wish the world would slow down and let us settle in to enjoy life with a simple day-to-day routine. Enough changes."

"Not all the changes are bad. I like your mustache." She played with the short curls around the corners of his mouth.

"That's one of the few good things I got from the time I was off at the war. I discovered I could grow a decent mustache. Now it seems to be the fashion. I enjoy being in fashion."

"It tickles me." Maggie smiled and kissed him.

"Yes. So many bad changes, but that's a good one." Oscar stroked her hair.

Maggie snuggled closer. "It's not the only good thing that's happened. We got married. That was good, right?"

"Yes, of course. But it was still a change. And my job with Van Kleeck's has been going well even though moving my work to the new factory up in Waterford was another change. I make a nice side income with the special little brushes I make. We're doing well. We're saving money."

"Could you be all right if there was one more little change in our lives?"

Oscar pulled back and looked at Maggie. She was beaming. "What?" he asked, starting to smile. Maggie's smile was contagious.

"We're going to have a baby. I expect the baby will be born next spring."

Oscar looked at Maggie, absorbing the news. "Oh! Maggie!" He kissed her.

Maggie leaned to him and touched his cheeks with her fingertips. "You're crying. Oscar, aren't you excited? Aren't you happy?"

"Of course. I just get emotional about these things. This is wonderful news." He paused, digesting the sudden turn in their lives. Then he continued, thinking as he spoke, the words flowing. "Next spring? We'll have to take Aunt Sarah's old room and get it ready for the baby. Have you told your parents?"

"No. I wanted to tell you first. Let's go over to see them after church on Sunday and tell them together. And we have to tell Addie and Rollo."

"Let's get up to Stub and Ann's orchard right away so we can tell them before the news gets there with Addie. As soon as she knows, she'll run up there to tell her brother. Why don't we find a time to go up there with Addie and Rollo? Then we can tell all of them at the same time."

Maggie hugged Oscar. "I've always wanted a big family with lots of children. Both of us have lost too many brothers and sisters. Now we'll have a little one of our own running around."

"I can't wait!" Oscar smiled.

Mother's Legacy

MY MOTHER'S PASSING LEFT many unanswered questions about my ancestors. As unreliable as her stories were, they had offered me a place to begin my search for the truth. And now, while cleaning out her house, I had access to everything stored there. I discovered it was filled with many real, tangible clues about my past that she had lost or hidden from me.

The immediate task after Mother's funeral was to go through everything in her house and decide who wanted to have which family heirlooms before my sister went home to France. We knew what to do with the obvious things: the furniture, the countless tabletop knick-knacks, and the jewelry. Those we divided among various family members.

After my sister returned to France, my nephew Daniel, his wife Anne, Debbie and I began what amounted to an archaeological dig. Mom never threw anything away. Her house was jammed with boxes and sacks filled with family mementos. We saved what we thought worthwhile. In the end, the real estate agent filled a two-ton container with trash as he prepared the house for sale.

What we uncovered was a quantity of old family things that were hidden away, stored in boxes, stuffed in closets, tucked in drawers. A basement storeroom was so jammed with old boxes there was only a narrow passage left for walking. I remembered how a few items like the old books, the brushes, and the wedding certificate kept turning up on the rare occasions when Mom allowed me to go through things with her.

Now, while digging through the closets and storerooms, we discovered a thick manila envelope stuffed with more of the MacMurray papers; more keys to the lives of Oscar and Maggie. There were pictures of them. There was a dark photocopy of Maggie's obituary from a New Jersey newspaper. There were old legal documents and old letters. And there was the long-lost packet of Confederate money. I saved everything though, given the urgency of closing Mom's estate, there was no time to give them the study they deserved.

In the basement storeroom we discovered an old cardboard box, taped shut and covered with a thick layer of dust and mouse droppings. As I was about to add it to the refuse pile I saw that it was labeled in black marker "Open this box immediately." It appeared that the box had been sealed when we moved from Virginia to Massachusetts in 1958. It was now 2015, fifty-seven years later. Of course I opened it immediately. "Don't I always do what I'm supposed to do?" I said to Debbie, smiling, remembering how often I didn't do what my Mom thought I should.

More books. Some were beautifully illustrated antique children's books I remembered Mom reading with me when I was a child. I noted that their publication dates meant they had probably been my mother's books when she was little. Her name was penned inside the front cover of one of them in a familiar flowing script, the same handwriting as in the Teachout Bible. I added these children's books to my stack of wonderful old books, along with the Doré *Idylls of the King* and *The Flowers Personified.*

In another smaller box I found one more old brush, this one a tiny perfectly crafted masterpiece with a curved, polished handle. There was also a thin book, carefully covered with a hand-sewn piece of red flowered fabric. Inside the front cover it was inscribed in careful penmanship, different than the writing inside my mother's books: James H. McMurray, September 3, 1883. My grandfather would have just turned eight. It was *The Second Reader* of the Popular Series, published by J. B. Lippincott & Co. in 1881, a primer with exercises for reading and writing, some short stories, and grammar drills. It was signed again with flowing calligraphic handwriting inside the back cover, James H. McMurray. Whether Oscar or Maggie wrote his name inside the cover, there was now no question that my grandfather James was undeniably a McMurray of Irish lineage as a child in Lansingburgh.

Now that the search for the truth about my ancestors was underway, I set all these materials aside. Piece by piece I began reviewing them. Along with my visit to Troy, my visits to Ancestry.com for genealogical research, and my Google searches of names and other leads, the story of Oscar and Maggie continued to reveal itself.

19

Idylls of the King
April 1872

A WARM SPRING BREEZE pushed past the lace curtains into the living room of the house on Ann Street. Maggie's once-tiny frame filled the space on the sofa next to Oscar. She was eight months pregnant with their second child. "Only a few more weeks," she said. "I'm ready for the baby to come now. I feel tired all the time. I can hardly get through a day without napping."

"That's all right," said Oscar, moving a cushion to the floor to give them more room. "We'll get through the birth. We did fine when Carrie was born, and this will be the same. Let's enjoy every moment together while we wait for your time to come. We'll count each day till it's time."

"I can't say this is enjoyable," Maggie fretted. "I'm never comfortable. But you're right. I'll get through it. I just want it to be over."

"You know what today is?" Oscar was smiling. He put his hand carefully on Maggie's shoulder.

"What?"

"It's our fifth anniversary."

Maggie shifted for a moment. She frowned, fretting. "I know that. Of course it is. I've been looking forward to it. But with the baby on the way and taking care of Carrie..." She rubbed her belly. Her eyes began to fill with tears.

Oscar massaged her shoulder. "That's all right. I understand."

"No, you don't. I was so hoping to do something special for our anniversary.

I wanted to have a nice dinner cooked for you. I thought maybe we could take a day and go on a picnic together. I had so many plans. But I've done almost nothing. I'm so sorry."

Maggie started to cry silently. Oscar leaned to her and gave her a light hug. "Maggie, Maggie. It's all right," he repeated. "We can go on the picnic after the baby is born. I don't mind cooking our meals."

"But I wanted to make it such a special day for you. I didn't forget, I just wasn't able to do everything I wanted to do for you. And you cooked me such a nice dinner tonight with the chicken and the potatoes. All I've done is sit around the house and take care of Carrie."

"You've done plenty. If I do the cooking and cleaning while you're pregnant, that's all right with me. And I've got a present for you."

Maggie pulled a linen handkerchief from her sleeve and wiped her eyes. "I don't know why I get this way. The smallest things set me off. Usually I'm stronger than this." She sniffed for a moment and tucked the cloth back into her sleeve. "I wanted to get you something too. Five years is an important anniversary. I had picked out a book for you. I had gone down to Albany running errands a month ago and I found this wonderful book. I didn't have the money with me to buy it right then so I had them set it aside. They're holding it for me in that bookstore you like."

"A book! How nice. And I can wait for it. Thank you. I got you some stationery and a new fountain pen. Here."

Oscar reached behind the sofa and produced a small package wrapped in white paper. Maggie peeled the wrapping paper open and set the pen and the sheaf of writing paper on the table in front of them.

"Thank you, Oscar. It's a beautiful pen, and I know I'll use the paper. I have my correspondence with the Women's Missionary Society, and there are our letters to your father and Sarah out in Minnesota. This is very nice. It's a wonderful gift." She kissed him.

"I have an idea," Oscar said. He took her hands and turned her to face him. "Saturday, if the weather's pleasant, let's get a carriage and go over to Albany as a family. We'll make it a family outing. I'll pack a lunch. We can have a picnic in the park and then go by the bookstore. What do you think?"

"I think it's a fine idea except for the picnic. I worry that once I'm down on the ground on the picnic blanket I could never get back up. But for the three of us to go to Albany as a family and stop at the bookstore... I would like that."

"We'll go for lunch in a restaurant then. I think Carrie's old enough for that. We'll have a wonderful time together, our little family of four." Oscar gently patted Maggie's belly.

Maggie smiled and hugged him, her arms around his shoulders, their bodies separated by her girth. "Till Saturday!"

*****

The carriage ride to Albany was leisurely. Oscar steered the rented carriage carefully over each bump in the road, taking his time, careful not to jostle his wife. The bridge crossing the Hudson took time too. Wagon and carriage traffic built up and slowed ahead of them and behind them. They were engulfed by noise, the rattle of the carriage on the cobblestones, the shouts of other drivers, and the huffing breath of the horses.

Carrie sat between her parents, pointing to things she saw, asking questions. "How far do we have to go? Is this the same river like the one we have in Lansingburgh? Oh, look at that big barge! What kind of a bird is that? When will we be there?"

Oscar and Maggie answered each question patiently. "We're almost there. Yes. This is the Hudson River. That's a blue jay. Almost there."

In Albany they checked the carriage at a stable and walked to a hotel. The hotel dining room was immense, nearly as large as the whole first floor of their house back in Lansingburgh. Gaslight chandeliers with frosted glass globes lit the room. The McMurray family was led to a table and seated. A white table cloth draped nearly to the floor.

"Oscar, this is so elegant. Can we afford this for lunch?"

"It's our fifth anniversary. We should do this. I set aside money every week from the specialty brushes I make in my little shop back of the house. And my wages with Van Kleeck are more than able to support us. We can do things like this on a special occasion like today."

"Why do they have this big cloth on the table?" asked Carrie. "It's so long. I can't see my feet."

"This is the way it is with fashionable people," Maggie explained. "When they dine, they cover the table with a tablecloth."

"Why? And why are there so many forks?" Carrie arranged the forks, aligning their tines so that the handles sloped from shortest to longest.

Oscar continued the lesson on fine dining. "It's nice, isn't it, the big white tablecloth? All the forks are for each course of the meal."

"What's a course?" Carrie asked, her brow furrowed.

"If we get salad before the main meal, that's a course, so that's a fork. Then there's a fork for the main meal. And if we get dessert, that's another fork."

"Why don't we use the same fork? I don't want to have to wash all these forks when we finish."

"That's all right. When we eat in a restaurant they wash the forks and dishes for us."

"Then I think we should eat in a restaurant all the time. I hate washing the dishes after we eat."

Oscar and Maggie laughed. Maggie explained to Carrie, "We only go to a restaurant on special days. This is because Momma and Daddy have been married for five years."

"That's a long time. That's longer than me. I'm going to be four next month." Carrie held up four fingers.

"That's right little one," Oscar said. "And right around your birthday Momma's going to have a new baby brother or sister for you."

"I hope it's a baby boy. I want a brother, and I can't wait for it."

"Neither can I," Maggie laughed.

After a beef stew lunch and apple pie for dessert, the family left the hotel. They walked the noisy streets to the bookstore. Carrie squeezed Oscar's hand, timid in the midst of so many people. Oscar guided Maggie with a steady hand at her back, making sure she wasn't jostled in the crowd. They paused at a corner to let the carriage traffic pass. Carrie looked around, overwhelmed, not talking and not asking questions.

When they entered the bookstore, a bell above the door tinkled. Carrie looked up and laughed. "They have a bell that rings when anyone opens the door!" She opened and closed the door two more times before Oscar quietly held the door closed to stop her.

Maggie explained, "That's so they know when someone comes in their shop."

"I want a bell on all the doors at our house. It's fun!"

A tall gentleman approached. He had mutton-chop sideburns and was dressed in a dark coat, a white shirt, and a small bow tie. He clasped his hands in front of him and spoke to Oscar. "Yes sir. May I help you?"

"Yes, but you should speak with my wife. She has made an arrangement here."

"Of course, sir. What may I do for you madam? You would want a book about flowers or gardening? Perhaps a novel. Something recent? I have copies of a new book, *The Innocents Abroad*, by a wonderful American author Mark Twain. It's like a new *Pilgrim's Progress*."

"No, I have selected a special book. You have it set aside for me? It's an illustrated copy of *The Idylls of the King*. My name is McMurray."

"Ah yes, that would be the Doré book. *The Doré Gift Book: Illustrations to Tennyson's Idylls of the King*." The clerk hurried to the back of the bookstore.

Carrie wandered away and returned with an illustrated children's book. "Can I have this?"

She handed the book to her father. Oscar looked at the book and checked the price. "Of course, little one. A book for each of my girls."

"Except that I'm buying you the Doré book," clarified Maggie.

"Ah, yes." Oscar nodded.

The clerk returned with *The Doré Gift Book: Illustrations to Tennyson's Idylls of the King*. He handed it to Oscar. "Here you go, sir."

Oscar didn't touch it. "My wife is buying it for me," he said, giving the clerk a stern look.

"Certainly." He handed the book to Maggie. Then he turned back to Oscar. "That will be two dollars," he said.

Maggie opened the small purse that hung by a strap from her wrist. "Here you are," she said, not smiling as she handed the clerk the money. "Could you wrap the book please?"

The clerk took her money, rang the brass cash register open and placed the money in the drawer. Then he began to wrap the big book in brown paper on the counter behind the register.

"Daddy, what about my book?"

Oscar took out some coins and gave them to Carrie. "When he finishes with Momma's book, you give him your book and this money." Oscar stood behind her ready to help if she needed it.

"Here you go Madam. Will that be all?" The clerk handed Maggie her package.

"I want this book." Carrie reached up with the book in one hand and the coins in the other.

"Of course, little lady. And would you like me to wrap your book too?"

"Yes, please."

He took the book and the coins and rang open the register again. "Here's your change," he said, handing Carrie a coin. Then he turned to wrap her small book the way he had wrapped Maggie's.

Carrie gasped, her mouth open, her eyebrows raised, staring at the coin in her palm. "Momma! Daddy! The man gave me money! Can I buy another book so I can get more money?"

"No sweetheart," said Maggie. She tried to lean down to give her daughter a hug. "That's just the leftover money from what Daddy gave you to buy the book."

"Is there leftover money every time we buy things?"

"I certainly hope so," Oscar laughed. "Today has been an expensive day."

"But worth every penny," Maggie said. "I haven't been out of the house much in weeks, and I still have several weeks to go."

Oscar smiled and gave her a light hug. "We'll do it again five years from now."

Carrie slept all the way on the carriage ride back to Lansingburgh, leaning against her momma's belly. It was late in the afternoon when Oscar dropped his two girls at the house and went to return the carriage to the rental stable. When he came back home, both Maggie and Carrie were asleep, reclining against each other on the sofa in the living room.

The Karcher Letters

AMONG THE PAPERS I found in Mom's storeroom were several letters from a woman named Dorothy Karcher, Mrs. Clark D. Karcher from Sandy Hook, Connecticut. In the early and mid-1980s, Mrs. Karcher had corresponded with my mother seeking information about the McMurray family. She shared research she did with the Rensselaer County Historical Society in Troy, New York, the same institution I had visited.

I read through the stack of letters from Mrs. Karcher to my mother and found copies of other letters with my mother's replies. From her letters, it seemed Mrs. Karcher believed she was a descendant of Anna Marie II, Oscar's youngest sibling. She might be more closely related to Aunt Addie and Rollo, since I would discover later they had moved to Connecticut. The information she shared with my mother substantiated much of what I had already learned about my family history.

After checking and noting that she might still be living at the same address as when she corresponded with my mother, I wrote her a letter, hoping she was still alive and able to assist me with my search. After several months the letter had not been answered, but it also had not been returned by the post office. She could still be out there.

My mother wrote back to Mrs. Karcher several times. Her first letter in

1982 corrected Mrs. Karcher, chiding her for referring to the family name as McMurray. It was predictable. She wrote a long section defending the Mac spelling and attesting to our Scottish heritage. Mom cited her aunt Carrie as the source of this fact.

> *... the family came to America about 1740 and settled in the area of Argyll, New York. It is logical that the MacMurrays would settle in Argyll because the Scots of that name live in County Argyll in the north of Scotland.*

My mother had always told me the MacMurray family came from Nova Scotia after leaving Scotland. I knew by now that Uncle Stub moved north to the McIntyre orchard in Argyll after the Civil war but my mother had never mentioned County Argyll to me. I wondered about the two stories, the one she told me when I was a boy and the one she shared with Mrs. Karcher in the letters. For a moment I almost began believing again in a Scottish heritage because of the convincing case Mom made. Then I rechecked my research noting all the McMurray spellings. I also noticed that in future correspondence with my mother, Mrs. Karcher tactfully dodged the issue by referring to our family as Mc/MacMurray.

My mother also referenced the "Teachout Family Bible" and listed the family births and deaths I had found there. She wrote in her letters that *Eugene A.* (her uncle) *used the 'Mc' spelling as an adult* though he is listed in the Teachout family bible as a MacMurray. She concluded her genealogy listing with:

> *My birth is the last entry and is in my father's very distinctive handwriting.*

That confirmed that all the bible listings were written with the "Mac" spelling by my grandfather James.

The last lines of my mom's first letter to Mrs. Karcher were the most telling.

> *...my father always used to warn Aunt Carrie when she got too enthusiastic about genealogy that if all you discovered was a horse thief you were fortunate!*

How many times had Mother said those exact words to me to steer me away from my research into the McMurray lineage?

Aside from her passionate defense of the "Mac" spelling, Mom's letters to Mrs. Karcher yielded other interesting bits of information about my family. Mom refused to share much family history with me once she had learned I was searching. It turned out that Mom knew a lot more about our family than she told me. The stories she shared with Mrs. Karcher were as deviant from what my research had revealed as were the few stories she had shared with me.

Of Oscar and Maggie's children, only Gene attended college and only for two years, a fact discovered on the internet. But both Eugene and James did very well professionally. What education they received, probably at Lansingburgh Academy, served them well. The preservation of so many books showed the family's dedication to reading and academic interests.

From Mom's letters I learned that Aunt Carrie was close to my mother. Carrie had no career, but most women at that time didn't work outside the home. She never married. Mom wrote:

> *Aunt Carrie was in many ways an anachronism, the genteel Victorian 'maiden lady' with many small talents and short-lived enthusiasms... She loved to read and read everything and anything she could get her hands on. But she was very disorganized and almost completely lacking in the domestic skills expected of women in her time. This lack earned her the disapproval and often the ridicule and scorn of both her own mother (Maggie) and mine (Grace, James' wife). Please don't misunderstand me – Aunt Carrie was a delightful person (she looked rather like the Fairy Godmother in Disney's Cinderella) and I was very fond of her... She read to me and played make-believe with me. She taught me to paint in watercolor, to identify birds and wildflowers, to enjoy opera, to make elegant doll clothes, to write stories and many other things.*

The comment about housework amused me. I remembered that my grandmother Grace believed a clean house and a devotion to housework were signs of virtue. I recalled how her annual Christmas visits to our house began with an inspection the moment she walked in the door. She would drag a finger along the top of a doorframe and check behind things in a cupboard, looking for dust. She would continue to inspect until her finger invariably came back dusty. Then she would shake her head and make a "tsk" sound.

About Aunt Addie and Uncle Sylvester Mom wrote of a family story in which:

> *Aunt Carrie sang a nursery rhyme about "Go tell Aunt Addie the old gray goose is dead." Aunt Carrie added that she really had an Aunt Addie.*

Mom said that her father James:

> *...used to tell me stories about visits to Uncle Sylvester's farm when he was a small boy. Uncle Sylvester was apparently a practical joker. The story I remember best was when he told Jimmy to jump up and down on the gate. When Jimmy tugged at the big gate all the turkeys that were roosting on the gate and nearby fence came flapping down on top of a much startled little boy.*

Mother also wrote that Aunt Carrie mentioned a Cousin Lottie. Could that be Charlotte?

Mother wrote to Mrs. Karcher that she had little information to share about Uncle Gene, noting *Uncle Gene never was much of a 'family' person.* But she went on to give many details about him, beginning with his marriage to Mabel Apgar in New Jersey, May 10, 1904 when he was thirty-two. Mom continued,

> *She (Mabel) and Uncle Gene were divorced probably about 1925. A few years later there was Aunt Bessie – Bessie Lambright McMurray and her son Howard Lambright who was a few years older than I. Howard kept the name Lambright until his late teens or early twenties when Uncle Gene wanted him to take the McMurray name and join the McMurray architecture firm.*

Mom then recited again her story about Uncle Gene changing his name,

> *... to use the 'Mc' spelling to please his Irish architectural clients because he designed several large Catholic churches, one of the most imposing of those is Sacred Heart Church on South Orange Ave., Newark."*

The architect for the Catholic Churches being the reason for Eugene "becoming Irish" is the same story she told me when I discovered the Mac/Mc puzzle. My research about Eugene found many references to him as a civil engineer, working for Sawyer Civil Engineering in Newark by 1890 when he was only eighteen. Searches revealed Eugene being awarded contracts to build roads and bridges in the area. He surveyed the house lot on Richelieu Terrace in Vailsburg where Oscar and Maggie lived in their later life in Newark, so he was working as a surveyor and civil engineer in 1897. There is one mention of him in a census record as an architect but no other evidence that he ran his own architectural firm or built Catholic churches. There is nothing wrong with being a civil engineer. Why change that fact to say he had his own architectural firm?

Mom concluded that Uncle Gene *had his father's regimental roster framed and hung in his home.* She mentioned later that she didn't know where the roster might now be.

She noted that little Edna MacMurray was born in Newark on June 6, 1891 and died less than a year later. Maggie was forty-three years old and we know that mid-life pregnancies and births are difficult, even today. It had been sixteen years since her next youngest child, James, was born. Oscar was forty-eight when the baby came. Edna must have been a sickly baby. She died February 29, 1892, just over eight months old. That series of events must have been very emotional for the whole family. Their other children were in their late teens and early twenties. Twenty-three-year-old Carrie most likely was still living at home with Oscar and Maggie. The boys were certainly living nearby if not also at home.

About her father James, mom wrote,

> *My father started working for the Prudential in his mid-teens and celebrated 45 years with the company in 1936 or 1937.*

Imagine him, right out of school, getting an entry level job and then working his way up with Prudential over the next forty-five years. Mom said that it was "Prudential Bank". Was there a banking division to Prudential at that time? Regardless, James did very well for himself. He married my grandmother Grace on May 29, 1920 when he was forty-five years old. They settled several miles from Vailsburg in Maplewood, New Jersey, an affluent community at that time. My mother, their only child, was born just over ten months after the wedding.

She added little else about her father except to note that she was very upset when he died suddenly during her first year of college at Mount Holyoke.

The census records and the pension documents show that Oscar and the family were McMurray's until Oscar's death in 1907. But James was calling himself a MacMurray by 1910, possibly sooner. Except in her obituary in the newspaper, Maggie was always a McMurray. Eugene never changed his name. Carrie followed James with the change. It appears that James was looking after his older sister even though she was thirty-nine years old at the time of Oscar's death. A proper unmarried woman like Carrie couldn't live by herself in that age. It looks like she stayed with Maggie for a few years after Oscar's passing. Then, possibly after Maggie's death, either Eugene or James had to look after her. She went with James.

It appeared that my mother knew a great deal more about our family background than she shared with me when I asked about our family history. Much of this family history, these stories, right or wrong, Mother shared with Mrs. Karcher in the letters but withheld from me. Why? Did her father James create this collection of myths about our Scottish heritage, about his brother Gene's name change and about Carrie? Did she believe her father, or did she know the truth but chose to continue her father's story? Maybe she was concerned that I was getting too close to what she knew to be the truth about our family. Now that she was gone, she couldn't talk with me about our family, but her letters gave me more information to support or refute what my research had discovered.

Disabilities, Pensions
and other Legalities

MRS. KARCHER'S LETTERS REFERRED to some legal documents she sent to my mother. I searched and found a thick stack of folded copies of legal papers. One set was Oscar's application to the war office in New Jersey for a disability "invalid" pension as a Civil War veteran first in 1897 and again in September 1904. He died three years later in 1907. He had just turned fifty-four when he first filed. The second set was a series of documents filed by Maggie shortly after Oscar died seeking a widow's pension in 1907, again from the war office.

The disability pension series offered new insights into Oscar. In 1897, he listed his occupation as brushmaker. He was still listed as a brushmaker when he filled out the second form in 1904. It confirmed the dates of his birth, and his enlistment and discharge from the 177th New York Regiment. It said that he lived in Lansingburgh from the end of the war until August of 1885 but noted a stay in Columbus, Ohio for a few months in 1870, 1871. Was this a visit to his father James and his second wife Sarah? Were they still living in Ohio? When they moved to New Jersey in 1885, Carrie was seventeen, Eugene was thirteen, and James was ten.

Oscar and his family lived in Newark at 93 Jefferson Street from 1885 until November of 1897 when he moved to Vailsburg, just west of Newark, a village that is today a part of Newark on the town line with East Orange.

The Jefferson Street address is only a block from the Passaic River, a working class neighborhood of small houses at that time. It is much the same today. In 1897, the McMurray family bought a house at 31 - 33 Richelieu Terrace in Vailsburg, three miles away from the Jefferson Avenue address. They were moving to a larger, more middle class home. They could have been renting the Jefferson Avenue home, but they had a mortgage and owned the Richelieu Terrace house.

On the pension form, Oscar described himself as being five feet four inches tall, weighing 145 pounds with blue eyes and gray hair. He explained the reason for going on disability as "Rheumatism and Catarrh in the head". Maybe his ability to continue with his brushmaking was limited, requiring the pension. Perhaps he had become a foreman and was no longer making brushes. Regardless, he lived twenty-two years after moving south to New Jersey. He was sick and on a disability pension for the last ten of those years. He would have suffered from a decade of stiffness and coughing.

Oscar was given the disability pension and collected it until his death in 1907. The record of his death gave me more information. His occupation was now listed as brushmaker, as it always had been, and also as "Celluloid," an occupation that I was unaware of. In her letters, Mrs. Karcher also questioned what Celluloid meant as an occupation. The death certificate indicated that Oscar died at his home and listed the cause of death as "Intestinal Nephritic," internal issues involving his kidneys.

The Richelieu Terrace address confirmed a location I had discovered in several other places. In her obituary in 1921, Maggie was also listed as living there. There is little record of what Maggie's life was like in those fourteen years after Oscar died. My mother was less than a year old when Maggie died.

Maggie's life was busy in the first years she lived in New Jersey. She attended a meeting of the Women's Home Missionary Society of the Methodist Episcopal Church in Boston a few years after 1888, when Mrs. Rutherford B. Hayes addressed the group. But the program Maggie tucked into *The Flowers Personified* notes that Mrs. Hayes died in 1889. Whenever Maggie acquired the program, it meant enough to her for to preserve it. Her membership in the Women's Home Missionary Society also points to her involvement with her church and with politics in an era when women did not yet have the right to vote.

To collect her widow's pension, Maggie needed to prove three things: that she was indeed married to Oscar, a war veteran who had collected his pension until his passing, that she had been married only to him, and that they had lived together until his death. Seeing the stack of documents she had submitted to prove these facts reminded me of the collection of forms I had gathered to settle Mom's estate after her death.

The first of the documents in this series stated that Maggie and Oscar lived at and owned:

> *a frame two story and half house located on two lots at 31 and 33 Richelieu Terrace, Vailsburgh Section, City of Newark... And the value of this property is Seven Thousand Dollars.*

The same paper also listed Maggie's personal property with a value of 400 dollars and mentioned that Oscar had left:

> *...her a Benefit Certificate in the Knights of Honor for the amount of Two Thousand Dollars, and when this is paid, it will require One Thousand Dollars to settle all outstanding bills including Doctor, nurse, undertaker, Cemetery lot and the claimant's household expenses since the death of the soldier.*

I was struck by the amount of money Oscar had amassed as a brushmaker. He owned a large $7,000 home, though further reading of the documents pointed to a $3,400 mortgage. That was an expensive home in the 1890s. He and Maggie had a $2,000 insurance policy if that is what the Knights of Honor money represented. And they had $400 more in cash on hand. For that time, they were a prosperous family. How could a brushmaker do so well? They had come a long way from the small house on Ann Street back in Lansingburgh. Was the key to their prosperity to be found in the conflicting Brushmaker and Celluloid listings as "Occupation"?

Maggie submitted several other documents to support her application for the widow's pension. Three were from people she asked to witness that she was married to Oscar and was never married to anyone else. One was completed by Royal Comstock who was 65 years old in 1907 and living in Rocky Hill, Connecticut. It was notarized in Hartford. The second was filled out by Sylvester S. McMurray who was 69 years old and still living in Argyle, New York. The third was from J. Henry Theberath, a thirty-nine-year-old man who lived in South Orange, New Jersey. It was wonderful to see that Rollo and Stub were still in contact with Oscar and Maggie.

I did a quick search for J. Henry Theberath, the third witness. Late in the nineteenth century he was a wealthy owner of a jewelry company in Newark that thrived because Mr. Theberath designed and patented numerous new jewelry clasps and fastenings. He was a pillar of his church, possibly also of Oscar and Maggie's church, donating thousands of dollars. He became the acting mayor of Vailsburg in 1908, a year after Oscar's death. The document he signed for Maggie was dated three weeks later than Rollo and Stub's. Maybe a lawyer told Maggie she needed three witnesses. She found a notable one with Mr. Theberath.

To prove her ownership of the house at Richelieu Terrace, Maggie submitted a handwritten legal document detailing the value of the house, noting the $3400 mortgage with the Protection Building and Loan Association of Newark, dated July 27, 1897.

> *The plot is on Richelieu Terrace a bit over three hundred and seventy-two feet from the corner of the intersection of the street with South Orange Avenue. It is a moderately big double lot, numbered 133 and 134 on a map of Hazelwood Park though the house is numbered 33.*

The map was *made by Eugene A. McMurray, Surveyor and Civil Engineer.* So in 1907, after Oscar's death, Eugene was a civil engineer, not an architect. And still a McMurray as always.

The final document I found was a dark photocopy of a newspaper clipping from 1921.

Mrs. Margaret J. MacMurray

> *Mrs. Margaret J. MacMurray, widow of Oscar E. MacMurray died yesterday at her home, 33 Richelieu Terrace. She suffered a stroke of paralysis last week.*
>
> *Mrs. MacMurray was born in Waterford, N.Y. seventy-four years ago. She resided there and at Troy until thirty-seven years ago when she moved with her family to this city, where she since has lived. She was a member of the South Orange Methodist Episcopal Church.*
>
> *Those who survive are: A daughter Miss Carrie M. MacMurray and two sons, Eugene A. MacMurray and James H. MacMurray, all of this city.*
>
> *Funeral services will be held tomorrow night at the home. Rev. Benjamin F. Dickison, pastor of Central Methodist Episcopal Church will officiate, assisted by Rev. Thomas M. Pender of the South Orange Church.*

I noted that Maggie and all her children were listed as MacMurray when she died in 1921. But all the legal documents showed the McMurray spelling. It became evident that the name change had occurred right after Oscar's passing in 1907. But perhaps only James and possibly Carrie went along with it. James must have submitted the obituary to the newspaper even though Eugene was older.

If James did indeed change the name and begin his systematic altering of records to assure that the family was MacMurray, it might have begun before 1920. He is still listed as McMurray in the 1920 census but is officially a MacMurray in the 1930 census.

My grandmother Grace Cooper married James on May 29, 1920 in Maplewood. In the pile of treasures I discovered in Mother's house after she died I found a booklet that was the official record of their marriage. In it there are several key details. The wedding was witnessed by Eugene A. McMurray—Mc, not Mac. Where James signed the certificate, his handwriting matched that in the Teachout Family Bible where all the names are MacMurray.

All the guests signed inside the little booklet. Among them, all listed on one page, are Margaret J. MacMurray, (Maggie), Carrie M. MacMurray, Eugene A. McMurray, and Mabel V. MacMurray who would be Eugene's wife, not yet divorced. Yes, they are all MacMurrays except Eugene. But looking carefully there are telltale marks and puzzling lines around the Mac's for Maggie and Mabel. They are similar to the altered spelling of the signature on the old drawing of the sailing ship Oscar drew when he was a boy. Whether or not Maggie had her name changed in the wedding booklet, I doubt that Eugene would stick with the McMurray spelling while his wife Mabel would write it MacMurray. Then again, they were divorced within the next five years.

Maybe I'm making too much of the different spellings. Leave it at this. My grandparents and my mother were MacMurrays. Oscar and Maggie and Eugene were McMurrays. Why there was a change, when, and how deep in the family the change went may always be in question.

Celluloid

THE ARRAY OF OBJECTS and papers I acquired in the hidden caches of treasure in Mom's house answered many questions. I was now sure about most of the details in the lives of my great-grandfather and great-grandmother, Oscar and Maggie. I had confirmed where they lived in Lansingburgh and later in Newark and Vailsburgh. I knew they had moved to New Jersey in 1885. But I didn't know why. I knew my grandfather James had been the one to change the name to MacMurray and that he did it after Oscar died. I knew he had painstakingly gone back through many documents and had written in the Teachout Family Bible to document the name change. And again I didn't know why.

I was puzzled by some of these new discoveries. The family had prospered after the move to New Jersey, far more than I would have suspected for a brushmaker. Maybe this was due to the additional income from Eugene and James when they started working. A civil engineer career for Eugene and a job with Prudential, possibly in banking for James, certainly would have helped the family. And what was celluloid?

I searched on the internet for Celluloid and was astonished at the answer I found. Celluloid was an early form of plastic discovered in Europe in the mid-nineteenth century. A German scientist learned that a mixture of nitric and sulfuric acids added to cotton produced a highly explosive material that became known as gun cotton. Predictably, this material found immediate military uses. Later its use became commonplace not as an explosive but as celluloid, a raw plastic. A safer material, a nitrated form of cellulose, was discovered and called pyroxylin. By 1860 chemists in the United States were working with a new pyroxylin made with camphor.

I was beginning to become bored with this story of early plastic. It didn't seem relevant to Oscar and Maggie's story. But the next piece of the celluloid chronicle caught my attention. A printer from Albany, New York, John Wesley Hyatt began working with pyroxylin in pursuit of a better billiard ball. Billiards was a popular game at that time and the Civil War had made it difficult to import elephant ivory, the traditional material for making billiard balls. A New York billiards manufacturing company proposed a $10,000 reward for an ivory replacement. In pursuit of this prize, Hyatt improved the process for producing pyroxylin. He was awarded a patent for the new process in 1870. He and his brother Isaiah went into celluloid production in Albany with the Albany Dental Plate Company in 1870. They were the Orville and Wilbur Wright of plastics.

New York investors backed them and, at the insistence of the New Yorkers, the Hyatt brothers moved production to a new factory, the Celluloid Manufacturing Company, on Newark's Mechanic Street. I checked a map and discovered that Mechanic Street is in what is now Orange, New Jersey, barely a mile from Richelieu Terrace, the eventual home of Oscar and Maggie. In the beginning, the Hyatts produced unprocessed blocks of celluloid in the factory. They sold the material to other nearby manufacturers who turned it into items that consumers would want. Brushes were a popular celluloid product.

This was an age of entrepreneurial tinkerers and inventors. Thomas Edison lived and worked right down the road. He was very aware of celluloid, and it was among the many materials he tested for his light bulb filament. Celluloid filaments burned up of course; remember gun cotton? Coated with silver, celluloid became the standard for early movie film. Newark had other inventors who helped bring prosperity to the region. J. Henry Theberath with his jewelry patents was among Newark's best tinkerers.

Fires and explosions were commonplace in celluloid factories. More than three dozen fires and explosions occurred in Newark in less than a decade, but business was booming. The Celluloid Manufacturing Company burned to the ground in 1875. They rebuilt quickly and despite the fire, the business was extremely profitable. By 1879 the company's profits were nearly $100,000 a year, and by the early 1880s investors were getting large dividends. Rival celluloid companies sprang up nearby. Newark became the celluloid capital of North America.

Pictures on the internet showed celluloid brush sets. Stories about celluloid often mentioned its use for brush handles. Today, antique stores have celluloid brushes with a distinctive amber or tortoise-shell appearance. That the Hyatt brothers, the pioneers of celluloid in the United States came from Albany, across the river from Lansingburgh and moved their business to Newark couldn't be coincidental. And there were the documents listing Oscar as employed in both brushmaking and celluloid. The pieces were beginning to fit together.

One article even stated that the Hyatts began diversifying their business into finished goods in the mid-1880s. I imagine the Hyatt brothers noted the profits of the manufacturers to whom they sold their raw blocks of celluloid. They also discovered that these companies were making brushes. They reflected on the brushmaking heritage back home near Albany up the river in Lansingburgh and Waterford. John Wesley Hyatt might have said, "We can make brushes too. We know brushmakers from back home." I imagine Isaiah responding, "Let's set up a brushmaking business here. With our profits we can lure some of those brushmakers down from Lansingburgh to Newark. We can make it worth their while."

The Move to Newark
1885

OSCAR SAT AT THE kitchen table in the house on Ann Street. It was late in the afternoon and the springtime sun still heated the kitchen. In spite of the warmth, Oscar felt chilled. He was frightened by a future he couldn't control, the bleak prospect of being out of work. Oscar's hands, still dusty from his day's work, rested on the table top. Fine sawdust from drilling and sanding brush handles speckled his sleeves.

"Where are the children?" he asked Maggie.

She turned from the counter where she was cutting biscuits from a rolled sheet of dough and wiped her hands quickly on a towel. "Upstairs in their rooms reading their books for their school work."

Maggie saw the dejected look on Oscar's lined face, his eyes focused far away, somewhere not in the room. She saw the slump of his shoulders. She noted that his hair remained thick and curly but was now shaded with tips of gray. He was still handsome, but she realized suddenly how both of them had aged.

Maggie put down the towel. "What's the matter?" she asked as she sat next to him at the table.

"Nothing. It's all right." But he looked up at her, his eyes intent. Then he turned away distracted. Maggie waited. She knew when he got like this he would take a moment before telling her.

Oscar shifted in the chair to face her directly. "The Van Kleecks let two more men go today," he said. "We're down to twelve brushmakers. We had almost thirty when business was good ten years ago."

"Why?" Maggie asked, understanding her husband's worry. "Why would they be letting so many men go? They let a man go last year at Christmas. And two others several months earlier last year. What is happening?"

"I suspect the Van Kleecks are losing money. It's not the way it was. Thirty years ago Lansingburgh and Waterford were booming. The Erie Canal made us a trading center. And people had a lot of uses for brushes back then too. People used brushes for everything. They had brushes for their boots, their clothes, their hats. There were brushes for their hair and their teeth. And horse brushes of course."

It was a litany of the many types of brushes he had recited often in past years. But things had changed. "Horse brushes are still a big thing, but people don't need so many different personal brushes anymore. Fashions change. Our business must be down and now the railroad has made the Erie Canal obsolete. This whole region isn't what it used to be."

"Are we going to be all right?" Maggie felt his concern. Recently, she had begun to worry as well.

"I don't know." Oscar shook his head and looked away from Maggie. He didn't want to worry her, but he needed to talk about his concerns. She always understood and made him feel better at times like this. "All I know how to do is make brushes. It's what my father did, what everybody in the McMurray family does. It's all I've ever done. I don't know any other trade. I know the Van Kleecks like me and like my work. I've proven myself. But if they go out of business..." He looked out the kitchen window at the fresh buds on the tree outside. He thought about the optimism he usually felt in springtime. That was missing this year.

"I know," Maggie said, sitting next to him, resting her hand on his sawdust-covered sleeve, comforting him with a touch. "I saw it coming when they let the man go back at Christmas. I've been praying ever since that everything will work out for you. For all of us."

"For you too," Oscar said, covering her hand with his. "And for our children. I need to make sure they get a good education. That they stay healthy and well fed. I see how it's been for the men who're let go. They all have moved from the region to find work somewhere else. I have no idea what sort of work they find. But I'm a brushmaker, and brushmaking may be a dying trade. I don't want to die with it."

"Oh, phsh!" Maggie gave a short laugh. "You're not going to die if you have to change trades. You'll be fine."

"How do you know? It's all I know how to do. I'm one of the best brushmakers but it's the only skill I have."

"You have other skills," Maggie said smiling, trying to cheer him up. "You're an artist. And you're a wonderful father. And an amazing husband," she added with a quick wink.

"Sure. But what if I can't provide for my family?"

"Everything will be fine," Maggie asserted. "I've been praying about it."

*****

A week later, Oscar began the long walk back home from the big wood-frame factory on the riverbank in Waterford. He had worked for Van Kleecks ever since he came home from the war except for the brief time when he had gone to Ohio, to help his younger sister Sarah get settled with her Otis relatives. He wondered how long he would be able to stay with the Van Kleecks. They were good people, and they had been loyal to him. But business was business. He had to trust in Maggie and her prayers. He had to push his worries from his mind and take each day as it came.

A man fell in, walking beside him as they approached the familiar bridge crossing the Hudson to Lansingburgh. "You're Oscar McMurray?"

"Yes." Oscar continued walking, but he looked carefully at this stranger who already knew his name. The man was fashionably dressed in a fine coat of light wool, dark striped trousers, a silk tie and a white shirt with French cuffs and a round collar. His shoes were well-made and polished. Oscar continued the conversation cautiously. "And who might you be?"

"My name is John Hyatt. I used to live across the river over in Albany but now I'm working down in New Jersey. Have you ever been to New York City? Or to New Jersey?"

"Yes, we shipped out to the war through New York City. New Jersey is right across the river, I believe. I didn't see much of New York. And that was twenty years ago, but I know a little about what the big city is like."

"That's right. Where I live and work in New Jersey isn't far at all from New York City."

"What kind of work do you do, Mr. Hyatt?"

"I have a factory that makes celluloid. It's a new material. We sell to businesses that use it for a variety of purposes. Some of them are making brushes with celluloid."

"Yes. I know of celluloid. From what I've seen, wood still makes the finest brushes. There's nothing like the look and feel of a finely made wooden brush."

"That's true." Hyatt paused, slowing for a few strides as they walked. "I've asked around town. People tell me that you make the best wooden brushes."

Oscar smiled. It was good to hear that he had such a fine reputation as a brushmaker. He wondered where this conversation was going. "Thank you, Mr. Hyatt. I appreciate the compliment." Oscar waited.

"That's why I've come to talk to you," said Hyatt. "We're expanding our business in New Jersey. I'd like you to consider joining us to be the foreman for our new celluloid brushmaking business."

Oscar nodded but said nothing. He strolled along with the well-dressed stranger, thinking, considering his answer. Hyatt allowed him the time. The two men continued together walking without a word for nearly a mile.

Oscar stopped. "I live a block over from here, so I'll be turning at the corner. Give me a bit of time to think about your offer."

"I know where you live. I went by your house two hours ago trying to find you and spoke to your wife."

"You spoke to Maggie? What did she say?"

"She said she would talk with you when you got home. She's a lovely woman and very devoted to you and your children."

"When do you need my answer?"

"I'm staying for a few days with relatives across the river in Albany. I'm hoping to hire four brushmakers before I leave."

"Very good. Can we talk further about your proposal tomorrow evening when I get home from work? I'll want to discuss this with my wife."

"Certainly. Till tomorrow evening." Mr. Hyatt reached out and shook Oscar's hand, showing no concern for the sawdust that fell from Oscar's arm onto his fine clothes.

"Till then." Oscar turned the corner and walked down Elizabeth Street and around the corner to his little house.

*****

Maggie was waiting at the door. "Did you meet a Mr. Hyatt?" she asked as soon as Oscar came in. Oscar could see the excitement in her eyes. She was beaming, her face lit with anticipation.

"Yes. He found me while I was on my way home. We walked together for a while, talking. Interesting fellow."

"Yes he is. He stopped here looking for you this afternoon. He's from Albany. Did he mention a job opportunity?"

"Yes. He proposed a job for me working with his company making celluloid brushes down in New Jersey. I'd be a foreman."

"What do you think?"

"I don't know. I've been with the Van Kleecks for so long. They've been loyal to me, and I owe them a lot."

Maggie nodded.

Oscar continued, thinking, working through the proposal as he talked, considering all the reasons the new job in New Jersey might be a mistake. "Your family is here, and it would mean moving, leaving them behind."

Maggie waited for Oscar to continue.

He squirmed as he sat down at the kitchen table. It was his favorite spot in the old house, a perfect place to think things through. "How can we afford to move? We would have to sell this house and take our children more than a hundred miles away."

Maggie interrupted suddenly with her own concerns. "We don't know our way around there in New Jersey. Where would we live? We'd have to find a new house in a strange new place. We would have to make new friends."

"That's all true," Oscar said, agreeing with her. "And I don't even know if this new celluloid brush business will succeed. I would be quitting my job here, and if this new brushmaking idea doesn't work out, we'd be stuck down in New Jersey with no job."

Maggie listened to his list of objections. Thinking it through though, the move made sense to her. It was the answer to her prayers. She carried on with their conversation. "Just a few nights ago we were worrying that Van Kleecks might not remain successful. And now this new job comes looking for you. I think you should take it."

"It's a risk. Would you be all right with leaving your family behind?"

"Yes. We can come back to visit, and they can come to New Jersey to see us. It would be fine with me. I just want you to have a good job and be happy."

"Mr. Hyatt said I would be a foreman. There is that. We would be starting a new brushmaking business, and I would be a pioneer."

"I suspect the pay would be good."

"Possibly. I haven't had a pay increase in three years. But food prices have gone up. A pay raise would be good. But how could we afford the move? We have our carriage, but we only use it when we need to and we have to lease a horse on those occasions to ride around town. Could we lease a horse here and turn it in there? Or would we have to buy a horse just for the move? How would we get all our furniture and belongings to New Jersey? Our carriage is barely big enough for the family with you and me on the front seat and the three children in back, and there's no room for all our belongings."

"I don't know. There must be an answer. Maybe Mr. Hyatt can help with those things."

"There are a lot of questions. There's so much to think about. It's sudden, and I haven't had time to think it through."

"Do you remember back during the Civil War?"

"Yes, of course."

"You didn't know if you should enlist or not. It took you several months to decide, but when you went off to war it all worked out."

"I don't know about that. I didn't get killed but I got sick. And my health hasn't been the same since then."

"But you got through that, and you're all right. This could be the same."

"I don't have months to think about it this time. Mr. Hyatt will be coming by to see me and get his answer tomorrow evening. I need to make up my mind quickly."

"Ask him questions," Maggie said, helping Oscar sort out his thoughts. "Ask him how much he will pay you. Ask him if he can help us make the move and find a new house in New Jersey."

"I could do that. If his offer is worthwhile, I might take the job. If he doesn't have answers to my questions I can always stay with the Van Kleecks."

"Yes you could. As long as they have work for you. Right now you have a job and an offer of a new one. You have options. That's all good."

*****

Oscar rushed home from work the next afternoon. He washed quickly and put on a fresh shirt. Then he sat waiting with Maggie in their cramped living room. The children had been sent upstairs to do their schoolwork, but they could be heard, whispering at the top of the stairs where they hid to eavesdrop on their parents' conversation with the well-dressed stranger.

There was a knock on the door. Oscar opened it and ushered Mr. Hyatt in. "Good evening Mr. Hyatt. Have you had a good day?"

"Good evening Mr. McMurray. Yes, it's been a very good day. I believe I may have two men already committed to come to work with me at my new brushmaking factory in New Jersey. They will confirm their plans with me tomorrow."

"Are they from Van Kleecks?" Oscar wondered if some of the others from Van Kleecks had also been approached. It might make the move easier if he knew some of his fellow brushmakers when they got to New Jersey.

Mr. Hyatt replied. "I'd rather not say until they've made their decisions. There are several brushmaking enterprises in town. That's why I've come back to Lansingburgh to recruit. I intend to hire the best people from the best brushmaking companies in America."

Recruit. Oscar thought about the word. It took him back to the war, when men were being recruited to go off to fight in the south. Too many of those men never returned. The idea disturbed him.

Mr. Hyatt continued. "You should know that this is a great opportunity for everyone who will be involved. This is the future of brushmaking. You'll be leading the way if you take the job I'm offering."

Oscar looked directly at Hyatt, preparing to judge the man's attitude when Hyatt answered the questions that had kept Oscar awake most of the previous night.

"How much would the job pay? I've been with Van Kleecks a long time, and I'm their lead brushmaker. I would be giving up a lot to start working for you."

"I'm aware of your time with Van Kleecks," Hyatt replied. "I've checked on your company, and I know they're struggling financially. But I want you to work with me. I need your expertise. I am prepared to compensate you very well." He handed Oscar a piece of paper with a number written on it.

Oscar looked at the number and tried to make sense of it. It listed his wage for a full year but in the moment he couldn't sort through the mathematics to break it into a weekly payment. It was obvious though that it was far more money than he had ever earned in any year over a lifetime of brushmaking. He handed the piece of paper to Maggie.

Oscar spoke slowly, calmly, keeping his face impassive, trying to remain composed. "This is a very generous offer Mr. Hyatt. I do have some questions, though. My family. I would need to move them to New Jersey with me. I would have to sell this house and find a new one. I would need to move all of our belongings."

"I understand. I want you to work with me," Hyatt repeated. "You would be an investment for me and for our business. I can help with all that. What do you need?"

"I have a carriage that we use for local trips here, around town. When we go out in the carriage I rent the horse so I don't have to keep a stable. And the carriage is only big enough for the family. I couldn't move all our furniture."

"Again, I understand. I can buy you a horse. You could keep it to get back and forth from your new house in Newark to our factory. And I plan to acquire a large wagon to move the households of the four men I hire. All of those expenses are the investment I am willing to make to start our brushmaking business in Newark. If you agree to work for me you would have to sell this house and find a new one, and I can help with all that too. I already have a house set aside for you to move into in Newark. I will do what I have to for you and your family to get moved and settled in New Jersey. What do you say?"

Oscar looked at Maggie. She was grinning. She looked at Mr. Hyatt and said, "I think he'll take it."

Oscar slowly began to smile. If Maggie was happy with the offer it must be good. He nodded. "This is all very new for me. I've never made a decision like this before in my life." He paused a moment longer. "How soon would I start?"

Hyatt got to his feet and adjusted his jacket. When he answered, he was smiling. "Let me hire these three other men. I'll see if I can get things finished here by the end of this week and move you all down to Newark next week."

Oscar stood with Maggie beside him. Mr. Hyatt reached out his hand and they shook.

Hyatt added the final touches. "A man will stop by tomorrow evening when you get home from Van Kleeck's. He is to help you arrange to sell your house and to talk about moving your furniture. I'll begin paying you your new wage as soon as you arrive in New Jersey. You can give notice at Van Kleeck's tomorrow. Here's a small sum to carry you over till you start working for me." Hyatt gave Oscar a thin pad of folded money. Then he was gone, out the front door, tipping his hat and striding purposefully down the street.

Oscar was shaking with excitement, anticipation, and fear. He called up the stairs, "Children, come on down. Your mother and I have some news to share."

*****

Monday morning, instead of taking his customary walk up the road to Waterford and Van Kleeck's, Oscar began loading furniture, wood crates of dishes and their personal family treasures into a large wagon. Maggie and the children helped. Two men, hired by Mr. Hyatt, lifted the heaviest furniture onto the wagon. Finally, they covered everything that Oscar owned with a heavy canvas tarpaulin. When the house on Ann Street was empty they drove the wagon to other brushmaker's houses to load their belongings next to Oscar's.

Oscar and Maggie packed their children into the back of their carriage. Carrie, the oldest at seventeen, sat between her younger brothers. Oscar and Maggie sat on the front seat. They left Lansingburgh mid-morning.

Three days later they were in Newark. Mr. Hyatt met them and showed them to a new house he had reserved for them near the Passaic River. The whole McMurray family worked all the following day filling their new home with their belongings.

Oscar found his way to the new celluloid brush factory, still empty but with benches and tables where he and his three men would work. He began his new career less than two weeks after he had met John Hyatt. He knew the other three Lansingburgh brushmakers; two were from Van Kleeck's. Everybody in brushmaking in Lansingburgh knew each other. They all adapted quickly to the new city and the new material. Within days, they were producing new celluloid brushes.

Edna: Remember Me
Newark, 1891 - 1892

MAGGIE SHIFTED UNCOMFORTABLY ON her bed in the cramped bedroom upstairs in the house on Jefferson Street. Hot, damp air pulsed through the window, flapping the lace-trimmed linen curtains, carrying the sour smell of the Passaic River two blocks away. Carrie sat by the bed pressing a cooling wet cloth against her mother's forehead.

"Daddy should be home soon," Carrie said. "It's late afternoon. He usually leaves work around four o'clock."

Maggie fretted. "I wish he would take the horse and carriage or catch the trolley up South Orange Avenue. Walking to work takes him so long."

"That's just the way he is," Carrie said with a resigned shrug. "He's always walked to work. Back when we were in Lansingburgh he walked to work."

"I know. And he's a man of habits. It does save a few cents for him not to take the trolley and that's important. But he doesn't have to walk anymore. He's so tired when he gets home, and he gets home late sometimes."

"Well, he's walking. He'll never change. He'll be here soon."

Maggie tried to sit up but fell back onto the bed. For a moment her face constricted with pain, the lines becoming deeper. She brushed a strand of graying hair back, tucking it into a tortoise-shell celluloid clasp. When she spoke, her voice was tired. "He needs to hurry. I don't know how much longer the baby will wait. I've been feeling terrible all day. I know this feeling from when you and your brothers were born. I don't think I can get up and fix you and the boys your dinner. I should, but I just can't. Anytime I try to get out of bed the cramping starts. The baby isn't due for another three weeks, but I think it's coming tonight."

Downstairs they heard a door slam and men's voices. Footsteps banged up the stairs, and Oscar came to the doorway, leaning on the frame briefly to catch his breath, his hat cradled in his arm. Gene and Jim huddled behind him.

"How are you feeling?" Oscar asked as he came into the bedroom. He kissed Maggie on her sweaty forehead. "The boys met me on South Orange Avenue and told me you're not feeling well."

"I've been cramping all day. I think the baby is starting to come. It's been sixteen years since James was born. That's a long time between babies but my body knows what's happening. It seems to remember how to do this."

"Should I send Gene to fetch the midwife?"

"No. I'll be fine. I've given birth three times before. I think I know what to do." She paused, feeling another cramp, her jaw clenching. "No, maybe you're right. Could Gene go find the midwife? And I don't think I can get out of bed to prepare your dinner tonight."

"I can take care of it. You need to rest." Oscar soothed her.

"But what about you and the boys? And Carrie? What will all of you eat?"

"We'll be fine. Carrie, could you help me with preparing dinner?"

"I suppose. I don't really know how to cook."

Maggie scolded. "You need to learn. This is a good time for you to start."

"All right Momma." Carrie sighed.

"I think I'll rest," Maggie said. Then she took Oscar's hand. "Why don't you and Carrie go downstairs and start dinner. I think we have some cheese and bread, and there's some corn left from last night and maybe a bit of leftover chicken. Check in the icebox. That's all we have. I wasn't able to get out to the market today so that will have to do."

"That's all right. Get some rest. We'll bring something up to you in a while."

They left Maggie resting and went quietly down to the kitchen.

*****

A bright dawn shone in through the curtains. Gene and James had slept through the sounds of Maggie giving birth in the master bedroom down the hall from their room. Oscar and Carrie had sat up all night on chairs they had dragged into the hall outside the bedroom waiting for a signal from the midwife that the baby had come. The delivery of the baby was surprisingly easy; Maggie's body went through the pushes, remembering the births of her first three babies. A tiny baby girl now snuggled, tucked in on Maggie's breast. They were both asleep. Carrie and Oscar helped the midwife take care of everything after the birth, cleaning up Maggie, the room and the bed.

Oscar hugged Carrie. "You did well helping me with your mother last night. She's going to be fine."

"But the baby's so small, Daddy. Is she going to be all right?"

"Of course. She's come early. That's why she's so little. She'll be fine. Now I'll go wake the boys and see if they can get word up to the Hyatt's factory that I can't come in today. Then I'll have them bring the doctor to check on your mother and little Edna too. Why don't you get some rest? Your mother might need you later today."

Oscar woke the boys in their bedroom. They sat up drowsily. Gene asked, "Did the baby come yet?"

"Yes," said Oscar. "Very late last night. She's a little girl. You have a baby sister. Edna."

"Is Mother all right?" James' face showed his worry.

"She's fine. But I'll need you two to help me a little this morning. I'm going to ask you to take the day off from work to stay with your mother. Gene, can you run up to my brush factory and let them know I'm taking the day today? Tell them I have a new daughter, and I need to stay home for just this one day. Mr. Hyatt will understand. He asked me yesterday if the baby had been born yet. He told me he'll allow me the one day when the baby comes. It's not customary but Mr. Hyatt likes my work. It's a benefit he'll allow me."

Gene looked at his father and spoke cautiously. "I'd do it Father. But I have to be at work at Sawyer's first thing this morning. I'm helping survey for a bridge we're building over the railroad line to New York. They're counting on me."

"Ah, all right. Jimmy, could you do it? You've finished with school for the year, haven't you?"

"Of course. I don't start work with the Prudential until July. I can take care of this for you."

The midwife came to the bedroom door, buttoning the cuffs of her sleeves over her thick wrists. "I've finished up here," she said. "But you should have your doctor come by to check on your wife and the baby. I'll be going now."

"That's good. Thank you," Oscar said. He paid her and sent her on her way.

"Jimmy, I might need you to run two other errands on your way to and from the brush factory. Could you stop by the doctor's office and tell them that your mother gave birth last night to a little girl? Ask if the doctor could stop by this morning and look in on her."

James nodded. He liked being asked to do these errands. It made him feel like an adult. He also enjoyed going out to South Orange and to Vailsburg, to the better neighborhoods with the finer new homes. "Of course. It's done. You said you have two errands for me along with my trip to the brush factory? There's the doctor's office. What else?"

"Yes. I need you to go to the market and pick up some food. Anything you want. We have nothing left here for meals for today or tomorrow. I'll give you some money."

"Can't Carrie do it? That's more something she should do."

"She was up all night with me and your mother. I think she's going to need some sleep."

"Oh. All right then. I'll buy something for us to eat. But she'll have to cook it."

"That's fine." Oscar gave James the grocery money. Then he returned to the bedroom and lay down beside Maggie and their new baby daughter. He fell asleep listening to Maggie's steady deep breaths and the quiet snuffling noises of his new little girl. He felt nothing but love.

*****

James took the horse-drawn trolley up South Orange Avenue. Riding the trolley was a pleasure he enjoyed whenever he could. Poor people, some of them Irish factory workers like the ones his father managed, walked alongside the trolley. They were headed to work and to their other menial appointments and errands. This morning as he rode in the trolley, James watched them walking, light cotton caps pitched back on their heads, carrying sacks with their lunches. When he started work at Prudential, James promised himself he would make sure he was viewed as a potential banker, dressing as well as he could and buying an inexpensive lunch to eat at his desk. He would never carry a sack of sandwiches to work. He would save his pennies and ride the trolley every day he could. The horse-drawn trolley wasn't expensive but it was a luxury only the well-to-do could afford. It required two coins, but today Father had given him money for food. He felt prosperous riding in the trolley while the workers walked.

Nearing Oscar's factory, he got off and walked the last several blocks down a side street to the looming Celluloid Manufacturing Company. The brush annex was a smaller factory next door where ten brushmakers were already settling into the day's work, cutting, grinding, and drilling brush handles out of blocks of the amber plastic.

"Is Mr. Hyatt available? I'm James MacMurray, Oscar's son."

One of the brushmakers, a lean Irishman, came to him. "Ah yes, Jimmy. I worked with your dad back in Lansingburgh. I remember you from up there. But you've gotten a lot bigger. You've become a grown man now, haven't you?"

"Yes I have. As a matter of fact, I'll be working with the Prudential starting in a few weeks."

"Well, very good for you. Mr. Hyatt's probably in his office over in the main building. You should go look for him there. Is everything fine with your dad and your mum?"

"Yes, everything's fine. Mother had a baby last night and Father needs to stay home with her today."

"Ah, well that's good news now isn't it? A boy or a girl?"

"It's a baby girl."

"Ah, a little girl." The man smiled, possibly remembering the birth of a daughter of his own. He clapped James on the arm. "Now that's wonderful. It's a special thing having a baby girl. You tell your dad that Eamon from the brush factory sends his congratulations. Now you should go look up Mr. Hyatt and tell him your news."

Eamon turned back to his brushes, and James walked around the corner and in the front door of the immense brick factory building. He had never liked coming to the celluloid factory. It was forever noisy, very hot, and smelled of strange chemicals. There was steam. It was the way James imagined Hell must be. There were offices off the entrance lobby to the right side and James turned in through the office door, grateful to be isolated from the heat, the noise, and the smells of the rest of the building.

Mr. Hyatt saw him as he came in the door. He stood from behind his desk and came around it to him, stretching out a hand to shake. "Jimmy McMurray! It's good to see you. If you're here, I suspect that you're bringing some good news."

"Yes, I'm James, Oscar's son," he said, stressing that his name was James, not Jimmy. "My mother gave birth to a baby girl late last night. My father says he needs to take today off. Is that all right?"

"Oh yes, of course. I told Oscar to do that. Is everything all right with mother and the baby?"

"I believe so. I'm going to stop by the doctor's office and have him come out to check on Mother, but I believe everything's fine."

"That's good. You tell Oscar I said congratulations. Now I expect you've got to get on your way. There'll be lots to do on a day like this. It was good to see you and tell your father I'll see him tomorrow."

Mr. Hyatt sat back at his desk looking through a stack of papers before James was out the door.

James walked back along South Orange Avenue to the doctor's office and shared the news with the doctor and his nurses. A nurse told him that the doctor would head out to the house shortly. Finally, James stopped and bought pork chops, bread, and milk in a heavy glass jug, and a bag of fresh cut beans. The family was set for dinner. There wasn't enough money left for him to ride the trolley so he walked the rest of the way home carrying his bag of groceries.

*****

When James got back to the house he found the doctor already sitting in the parlor with Oscar and Carrie. He put the meat and milk in the icebox and came back to join them.

"Her lungs are weak," the doctor said. "It happens sometimes when the baby is premature."

Oscar's face was gray. He sighed and leaned back in his chair, running his hands across his hair. "And Maggie? Is she all right?"

Carrie sat stiffly, listening but not reacting. Her eyes couldn't look at the doctor or her father. For a moment she glanced at James. But she began to tear up, her eyes glistening, and then she turned away.

The doctor continued. "Maggie is tired. I expect she's had a long night and giving birth is always hard on the mother, especially at her age. But she'll be fine. We just have to watch baby Edna. She's tiny and weak."

"What can we do?" asked Oscar.

"Take care of Maggie. Rest will be all Maggie needs. As for the baby? Give little Edna time. Usually when the baby comes early it's the first six months that are critical. Look after her for the next few months. She needs fresh air for her lungs to develop. Then she'll probably be fine as well."

"What should we watch for?"

"Call me if she starts having trouble breathing. Her lungs need to be stronger. But like I said, it's the first six months. She'll be out of the woods after that."

Oscar nodded. No one asked what might happen if Edna struggled during the six months. But it was on everyone's mind.

*****

It had been three months. Each day Edna became stronger, but she still had days when her breathing was labored, particularly when the heat and humidity made it hard for even healthy adults to take a deep breath. It was sunset, and Oscar and Maggie sat with their children on wooden chairs in the back yard, seeking a cooling breeze from the stagnant Passaic River.

"When do you start back to school?" Oscar asked James.

"I don't go back this year. I'm working for Prudential now," James answered.

"I thought that was just a summer, temporary sort of a job. Something to gain experience."

"That's how it started but they like my work. I'm making a good wage. They want me to stay on in accounting. Here, look at my pay check. They promoted me, and now they pay me with a real bank check, not just cash like they pay the regular workers." James took the paper check from his pocket and proudly showed his father.

"Well, good for you," Oscar said as he looked over the check. "They're paying you almost as much as Gene's making with the engineering company, and he's been there two years now."

James smiled. He reached for his paycheck, but Oscar still held it, looking at it with pride in what his two boys were doing.

Oscar continued. "Gene's getting his own room across town in a few weeks. Are you planning to do something similar?"

"No, not yet. I figure I'll stay here for a while. I'll contribute a few dollars each week to help you out. But I'd rather start saving money, investing it at the bank."

"That's a good idea. Gene, it will seem empty when you move out. Even with Carrie and baby Edna here. I'm glad you'll stay a while longer, Jimmy."

"Of course."

Oscar took another look at James' check. "They spelled your name wrong on your check. Do you think you should have them correct it?"

"Did they? I don't know. It doesn't really matter. I'm planning to open a bank account there next week. It would be a bit of a problem for them to change my name on the payroll. But they'll accept my check into my account as it is since I work there. They know me."

Gene spoke. "They spelled your name wrong? How?"

"They added a letter." James, distracted, looked away. "They have me listed as MacMurray with an a, not McMurray."

"Well, we're McMurrays," Oscar stated. "You should have them fix it."

"Sure."

"And you should consider continuing with school. Perhaps you should think of going to college. The money's good to have, but an education is more important. You can never learn enough."

"But Dad, I'm already getting promoted at the bank. I'm smarter than all of the other summer temporary people. They want me to stay."

Maggie bounced Edna on her lap and unbuttoned her dress to nurse her. "Let him go, Oscar," she said. "He's got a good thing started at the Prudential. He can always continue to read books and learn while he works there. He's got a good job. He should keep it."

So it was settled. What Maggie decided was the way things were in their house. James continued working at the Prudential in accounting and the misspelled name was forgotten. At least for now.

*****

It was Christmas morning, and a cold sun was shining. Gene had come across town from his apartment to join the family for the day, partly to celebrate and exchange gifts but also to help Oscar and Carrie prepare Christmas dinner. Maggie's time was consumed with baby Edna. Gene noticed as soon as he came in the front door that the house decorations weren't out as much as they were in earlier years. It was obvious there had been no time for the usual Christmas gaiety. Then he saw his mother sleeping on the sofa with Edna bundled next to her.

He whispered to his father, "How are they doing?"

"Your mother is very tired. She hardly sleeps at night. But she'll be all right. The baby's another matter. She can't breathe. She's fussy a lot and cries. It's hard on all of us but mostly on your mother."

"How did the doctor visit go last week?"

"He's worried. He says Edna's still very weak. Her lungs just haven't developed. They aren't as strong as they should be. And with the grippe that hits everyone in the winter..." Oscar's voice trailed off.

"She'll be fine," Gene asserted, but his tone lacked confidence. He patted his father on the shoulder.

"I hope so. But I get sick every winter. I get all rheumy every year, and I worry that I'll give it to Edna."

"Is there anything the doctor can do? Isn't there something we can do for her?"

"I don't know. The doctor doesn't have an answer. We'll take care of Edna as best we can and pray."

*****

Seven weeks later Edna was desperate for breath, fighting the grippe, fighting through every moment. She wasn't crying; that took too much air and too much of her minimal strength. She fell asleep as she did every night bundled close to Maggie. Oscar had taken to sleeping on the sofa in the parlor to give his girls more room in the bed and to prevent his chronic runny nose from infecting Edna.

160

Toward dawn he woke to a quiet sound from upstairs. He tiptoed up the stairs and looked into the dark master bedroom. Maggie was propped sitting in the bed holding Edna close, her arms wrapping her. The little girl snuggled against Maggie's breast the way she always did. Maggie looked at Oscar and quietly caved in, crying.

"She's stopped breathing. Sometime during the night she just stopped breathing. Oh dear Oscar, our little baby girl is gone."

Oscar sat close to Maggie and pulled her to him. He held her, he tried to soothe her, but there were no words he could say to make this right. Carrie came quietly into the room. Then James. The four of them sat together in silence, unable to speak.

Slowly daylight filled the room, crawling past the drawn shades. At last Oscar spoke. "She was a little angel that we had in our lives for a few beautiful months. Now she's back with God in Heaven."

Maggie smiled, though she was still crying, and kissed the top of Edna's head. "She never knew anything about the world except the inside of this house and what she saw on her few brief trips outside to the doctor's office and church. I know she liked the sunshine."

"We had her baptized," Oscar said. "She's in God's hands."

"For that we can give praise," Maggie added. Still she was inconsolable, clinging to their baby.

"It's not right!" Carrie shouted. "She was just a little baby. Babies shouldn't ever die. It's not the way things are supposed to be."

Oscar reached for his daughter, resting his hand on her shoulder. "No, it's not right. But it's the way things are. When I was a boy, I lost two of my little sisters in one year. It happens."

"Well it shouldn't!"

"Enough!" Oscar shouted, stopping Carrie, silencing the room.

Oscar let the room settle. Then he spoke quietly. "Jim, get a bite to eat. You need to keep up your strength. And then could you run out to the doctor's office? The doctor can take care of whatever they do when someone dies. And Carrie, I need you to go over to the church and find the pastor. Tell him what's happened and see if he can come by the house. And one of you has to let Gene know, too. I need to stay with your mother this morning."

James was up and out of the room, off with his assignment. Tomorrow he would inform his supervisor at the bank why he was missing work today. This was more important. "I'll tell Eugene," he called over his shoulder as he left. "He lives right on the way to the doctor's office."

Carrie got up more slowly and leaned over, kissing both of her parents before she left. Oscar remained sitting on the bed, his arm around Maggie, numb with shock, unable to sort out his thoughts.

Maggie leaned to him for support. Together they held Edna. Oscar added one more thought as they waited for the children to return from their errands. "Mr. Hyatt knows how weak little Edna has become. I wouldn't be surprised if he figures out what happened when I don't come in. He'll understand."

*****

James rushed out into the frozen white dawn without eating. He hurried to Eugene's apartment and caught him before he left for work. His words gushed out, giving Gene the story as succinctly as he could. "Edna died last night. She was with Mother, and she simply stopped breathing. I'm going to get the doctor right now. Carrie's going to get the pastor. Once I've told the doctor what's happened I'm going back home to be with Mother and Dad and Carrie. I can't think about going to work today. I couldn't concentrate if I did."

Gene nodded, his face grim, his eyes averted. "All right. I'll come by when I get out of work. I think at times like this we need to be together as a family."

The two brothers gave each other a cursory clap on the shoulder and separated, Gene heading off to work at Sawyer Civil Engineering, James turning toward the doctor's office.

When Eugene came into the office, his boss, Harold Sawyer, noticed his distracted attitude, the way he moved aimlessly as he gathered his maps and surveyor equipment. He saw Eugene's deadpan face and set jaw. He came to him. "How are you this morning Gene?"

"Fine I guess."

"You don't seem like yourself. Is everything all right today?"

Eugene paused, then, busying himself with some rolled maps, averting his eyes from Sawyer, he replied. "I don't know. I guess not. My baby sister passed away last night. She was only a few months old. I expect my parents are having a rough day."

He looked up stone-faced. He wouldn't let himself cry.

"Gene," Sawyer said, resting one hand on his young employee's shoulder. "You should go home. Be with your family today. That's where you belong." He took the maps from James and set them on a desk.

"Don't you need me today?" asked Eugene. "What about the work we're doing up at Hoboken? I can stay if you need me."

"We'll get by. Go. Take the day. Let us know about the funeral. This is what's right."

Without a word Eugene pulled his jacket on and started for home. His mind was chaotic. He walked several blocks then turned into a small park, found a bench and sat down. Young mothers sat on other benches watching their children playing. A lanky girl, wearing a wool coat, ran squealing from a smaller child. Her long legs carried her away from the chasing child. Knee-socks flying, the taller girl dodged around a tree but was caught on the other side by the little one.

"Tag! You're it!" More squeals. More laughter.

Eugene thought about Edna. He remembered how Edna would giggle when he tickled her tiny tummy. Edna loved to giggle. He thought about how she struggled to breathe and about how small she was.

"Today is February 29, 1892. A leap year, a day that only comes once every four years. 2-29-92." Eugene thought about the numbers. He usually found comfort with numbers, with the logic, the exactness, the predictability of the mathematics, the patterns, the geometry, the finite boundaries he derived from the numbers. He thought of basic surveying problems; measuring the exact length of a new street, defining the angles at an intersection, finding the perfect berm from the center of a paved road to the curb. There was no relief in the numbers today. Edna was gone. There were no numbers, no patterns, nothing predictable about it. It made no sense.

He leaned forward on the bench, elbows on his knees, with his head in his hands, his fingers threaded together, shielding his face from the children, the young mothers, the passersby. He cried silently.

After several minutes he stood, took out his white linen handkerchief, and wiped his nose and eyes. Composed again, he took a deep breath, straightened his jacket and started for his parents' home on Jefferson Street. He needed to be there.

*****

James left Eugene's apartment and walked to the doctor's office. He realized as he entered how little time had passed since the last time he was there on the day Edna was born. He told a nurse what had happened. She whispered to James that the doctor was with a patient but that he would go to the McMurray house within an hour. James thanked her and left. His errands for the morning were finished. He turned toward home.

Out on the street James suddenly felt hungry. It was now mid-morning, and he had hurried over to Eugene's without breakfast. He found a small restaurant on a corner along the way home, went in and sat at a table. When the waiter came James ordered a full breakfast: eggs, sausage, English muffins with jam and a cup of coffee. Most mornings a piece of toast was sufficient before he went to his office at the Prudential. Today he was very hungry. He couldn't explain why.

He ate slowly. When he was done, he left money on the table; enough to cover the cost of the food and a full dollar extra for the waiter. Life, he now knew, was far too short to worry about every penny. The waiter deserved some extra compensation.

James gave the waiter a wave and walked out onto the street. He had only walked a block further toward his house when he turned a corner and began striding along a side street, heading alone away from home. For the rest of the morning he walked without thinking, up and down strange cold streets, through neighborhoods where he had never been. His mind was a void. Finally, exhausted and chilled, he found his way back to the house and his small family.

*****

Summer evening sun washed through the front window from Jefferson Street. Trapezoids of fading light, stained faintly lavender by panes of old glass, touched the lace-trimmed curtains and the plants that lined the window. Thick new rugs covered the wide wood flooring. The parlor smelled of flowers. Oscar sat embracing Maggie, listening to Carrie play their new upright grand piano. They had no idea the name of the piece she played or who the composer might have been. Something European and almost contemporary, perhaps Chopin or Liszt, they guessed. A song without words.

Maggie tucked a trailing bit of hair back from her face. Her hair, Oscar noticed, had become shockingly white, without any trace of color. Her face appeared smooth in the evening light but webbed with fine wrinkles. She had aged dramatically since Edna's passing.

"She plays beautifully," Oscar said with pride. "It's such a pleasure to listen to her."

"Yes. I think she enjoys playing as much as we enjoy listening to her," Maggie said. Then she added, "Music is helping me move on from Edna's passing. It comforts me."

Oscar rubbed her shoulders, massaging the tense muscles gently. "That's good. This has been a hard time, the past few months through the spring. With Gene gone and now Jimmy moved off on his own, the whole house feels empty."

Maggie sighed. "And with Edna's death. I lost my brother, my James Henry, when I was young. But it's not the same as losing our own little girl."

Oscar nodded, thinking of the many deaths he had seen, including his own father, also named James Henry, just four years ago. The news had reached Oscar from Minnesota too late for him to go to the funeral. "Yes, I know,"

164

Oscar said. "My two sisters got the fever and died in the same year when I was little. But you're right. It's different to lose a parent or a brother or sister. It's just not right to lose a baby."

Maggie forced a smile. "Through it all I haven't lost my faith in God. He does things for a reason and He knew what was best for little Edna. But I don't understand it. I still miss her terribly. I feel like a part of my body has been torn away from me."

Carrie finished playing, folded her Scribner music book closed on the piano, and swiveled on the round stool to face her parents.

"I talked to a friend of mine. She's a girlfriend from church," Carrie said. "She volunteers sometimes at a doctor's office, and she knows about these things. She told me that it helps to do something, anything, just for there to be some activity to help us remember the one we've lost."

"That's very sage advice," Oscar said. "That's partly why we have funerals; to commit the baby's soul to Jesus, but also to help us find some peace with it. Did you do anything Carrie?"

"Yes." Carrie paused, deciding whether to tell her parents what she had done. "I've written poems about Edna. I wrote about what she was like, about what she thought of the world and of all of us. We all certainly loved her. And I know she loved us too."

"Could we read your poems?" asked Maggie.

"I don't know," said Carrie. She shifted on the piano stool, swiveling side to side. Her shoulders hunched. "I don't think they're good. And they're private, my own personal thoughts."

"That's all right, then," said Oscar. "If they helped you make some sense out of this. If they helped you come to terms with it and feel better, that's good. That's enough. Keep the poems for yourself."

Carrie nodded. "You should do something too, Momma. It does help."

"I've done some things to take care of it. Prayers of course. And private things."

"I've prayed as well," Oscar said. "I'm feeling better." Then he forced himself to brighten. "Let's go set up supper for your mother." He reached out and held Carrie's hand for a moment. Then he and Carrie went to the pantry to prepare supper. During the weeks after Edna's death, they had become the regular cooks for all the meals. With guidance from Oscar, Carrie was learning to cook. Maggie would have been a better teacher but she enjoyed the respite and loved watching them working together in the kitchen.

Maggie let them go. She went up the stairs to the master bedroom and opened the cabinet in the small nightstand beside the bed. She took out *The Flowers Personified*, laid it on the bed beside her, opened the book, and removed the narrow pink silk ribbon she had snipped from Edna's baptismal dress. With it was the needlepoint strip she had completed only the day before. Maggie trimmed the strip with scissors to the exact width of the pink ribbon. It only took a few stitches with pink thread at either end of the needlepoint to attach it to the ribbon. When she was finished Maggie knotted the thread and bit it to break it off. She held up the ribbon and assessed her work. It was good; Edna's pink ribbon and the needlepoint words, "Remember me" in blue letters. Maggie opened *The Flowers Personified*, kissed Edna's ribbon and laid it gently between the pages. It was preserved forever now along with the flowers, leaves, and other special keepsakes from significant moments in Maggie's life.

"Remember me." Maggie closed the book carefully, being sure not to wrinkle Edna's ribbon. Then she placed *The Flowers Personified* back in the nightstand and closed the cabinet door. It was time to go see what Oscar and Carrie were cooking for supper.

Life on the Prairie and
Back Home in the East

DEBBIE AND I HAD been married a year when she took me to her family's farm outside of Miller, South Dakota. This was where Debbie's great-grandfather had homesteaded, living in a sod house, breaking the prairie grass and soil for the first time to put in crops. Debbie told me the traditional family stories and showed me the shallow hole that remained where her family had built their soddy next to Turtle Creek.

The expanse of the prairie was overwhelming. I had never spent much time in the west, and this wide open terrain was new to me. From the second floor windows of her family homestead built on the farm near the hole where the old soddy used to be, I could see the street lights in Miller fifteen miles to the west. The land was absolutely flat with barely any trees. Roads were laid out through fields of wheat and corn following compass readings of due north-south. There were crossroads, mostly gravel, heading east-west, exactly a mile apart. I went on a ten-mile run from the farmhouse, running past fields of grain, south for a mile and a half to a dirt road, then west two miles, a right turn to go north three miles, a turn back east for two miles, and then south back to the farmhouse. Looking across the fields, I was never out of sight of the three-story house and the adjacent barn. It was as boring as an hour long run on a treadmill.

This was where Debbie's father had been raised. Her grandparents still lived in the farmhouse Debbie's grandfather and great-grandfather had built. The first evening at the farm, I sat at the dining room table after dinner with Debbie's father Merlin and her grandfather Harold. Debbie, her mother Dee, and her grandmother Ethel were engaged in animated activities in the kitchen, preparing plates of pie for dessert. Traditional roles still prevailed on the farm in South Dakota.

Harold leaned forward, his elbows widespread on the table top. He was a large man, well over six feet tall and still strong after decades of farm labor. His thick hands had knuckles swollen with arthritis. Harold produced an old black-and-white photograph on heavy card stock paper. He gave me the picture and asked, "What do you think of that?"

I saw a small man standing at the head of the immense mass of a cow. The man held a thin strand of rope leading up to the animal's nose. I could see the edge of a barn in the background, the same barn that still stood next to the farmhouse where we sat.

"That's a big cow," I said, answering Harold's question.

"Cow? That's not a cow! Look right there," he said, pointing at the beast's hindquarters. "That thing hanging there? That's not an udder. This is a bull. This is Hummerdale. He was our prize stud bull back in the twenties."

Eastern city-slicker greenhorn that I was, I looked more closely. Yes, Hummerdale was undeniably a bull. "That's a big animal, that bull," I said, correcting myself, stating the obvious.

"Big? Yes he was. He was well over two tons. He won prizes. And he was daddy to a whole lot of other prize winners. You should have seen Hummerdale Two. He was bigger."

"What's with the man standing there in front of Hummerdale?"

"That's me," answered Harold.

I looked again. The man in the photograph was much younger than the Harold who sat before me, but, yes, it was he. Harold was tall, but Hummerdale towered over him.

I decided to ask another dumb question. "Why are you holding the rope?"

"That goes to a ring in Hummerdale's nose. That's how I control him. That's how I make sure he doesn't wander off when we're taking the picture."

My leg was being pulled but I stumbled on. "You control him with that? I can't imagine why a big animal like that would stop if you pulled on that little rope. How could you stop Hummerdale just by tugging on the rope if he decided to walk away?"

"Oh, you're right," Harold answered. "If Hummerdale got a notion to walk past me I'd let him go. I'd drop the rope and wait."

"So why even bother with the rope? Hummerdale can do whatever he wants to do."

"Well, the rope makes Hummerdale believe I'm in charge."

"So how could you really stop him if he decided to go somewhere?"

"Like I said. I'd drop the rope and let him walk on by. Then, when he was just past me, I'd grab him by the tail and yank on it and flip him over on his side. That'd stop him."

Harold, straight-faced, demonstrated how to do it by making a motion with his hands like he was flipping Hummerdale. I saw Merlin grinning, his lips closed, stifling a laugh. Grandma Ethel rushed in from the kitchen bringing us plates of pie. Debbie and her mother followed with more pie. Ethel fussed, "Oh Harold! Enough of that nonsense. Telling Debbie's husband your stories about Hummerdale. Making him believe God knows what. Let it go and eat your pie."

Harold was like that. He took me out on drives through the farms at dawn, speeding through the fields on dirt roads, dust flying in a rooster tail behind us, waving to other farmers as they checked each other's crops. We went into Miller to a livestock auction and down to a hardware store in Huron "to pick up a part for the tractor" but really so we could swing by Kentucky Fried Chicken and get a bucket we could share in the park under the cottonwoods by the river. He told me more stories. I believed some of them, and I understood where Debbie's father Merlin got his gift for all his Navy stories.

During the depression, when the dust bowl wiped out the farm, Harold and Ethel loaded Merlin and his brothers and sister into the car and drove west to Portland, Oregon looking for work. They stayed there until after World War II when the weather improved and they were able to return to the farm. Merlin has boyhood stories about getting into mischief in Portland. His teenage stories take place back in Miller and on the farm. Then we get the Navy stories.

The depression treated my mother and her family in New Jersey very differently. Her father James had done very well with Prudential, working his way up over more than forty years. The MacMurrays had a fine house in Maplewood, several miles from Vailsburg. They had a summer house on a hill above Culver's Lake, an hour farther west of Maplewood and Vailsburg near the Delaware Water Gap. I have seen photographs of my mother as a little girl at the house on Culver's Lake.

They also spent time in the summer at Ocean Grove, New Jersey, living in a village of "tent-houses", a part of the Methodist Church Camp movement. The wood-frame, gingerbread-trimmed houses were painted the pastel colors of Easter eggs and roofed with white canvas. Mom took me there when I was very young. I remember it because it was my first experience with both salt water and sunburn. I also recall my mom relating stories about the long days in Ocean Grove when she was a girl, when they could do nothing on Sundays but attend church and prayer meetings. She told how there was no alcohol or tobacco allowed in Ocean Grove and that there were strict rules about what could and could not be done at the beach. Mom also talked about that sinful place a mile north of Ocean Grove: Asbury Park. She had pastel portraits of my sister and me when we were little, done by an artist on the boardwalk at Asbury Park. Portraits were acceptable, not a sin. They were still hanging in Mom's house when she passed away.

When she was a teenager during the depression, her father and mother wanted to take my mother on a "tour of the continent," something girls of wealthy families did in that era. That meant Europe, but World War II was brewing and it wasn't safe to go there. Instead, my grandmother Grace, my grandfather James, and my mother went west on a train for several weeks. They visited some of the famous western national parks, Yellowstone and the Grand Tetons. They saw buffalo, antelope, and other wild animals. They toured the Dakotas too, where Debbie's father had lived. Their paths wouldn't have crossed with Debbie's family since Harold and Ethel were still working and raising Merlin and their other children in Portland. Debbie's family didn't return to the Dakotas for several more years.

The depression treated the two families very differently. Years later, Debbie and I met, but that's another story. Our marriage merged the two families and their stories.

The Move to Vailsburg
Newark, 1897

IT WAS A WARM day for May, the air stagnant, still and thick with humidity. Eugene and James had come to join the family for Sunday dinner in the tiny backyard of the house on Jefferson Street. After church, Maggie directed her boys to set up a table and chairs under the trees. With Carrie's help Maggie served the meal: a beef roast, potatoes, and green beans with brown curls of fried onions, Oscar's favorite. Oscar sat in the sunshine at the table, coughing quietly. Maggie waited for the coughing to subside and then led the family in prayer. They were ready to begin dinner.

As the food was passed around the table, Oscar coughed again, red in the face this time, his body wracked by the violence of the spasms. He stopped and, gasping for breath, pushed his plate away.

An anxious Carrie placed her hand on his back. "Daddy? Are you all right? Can I help you? What can I do?"

Oscar blew air out slowly and sucked in a new breath, wheezing. He held the breath then pushed it out through pursed lips. His eyes were closed. "I'm fine. Just fine. I usually get the grippe in the winter. But now I'm always congested, even in the summertime. I don't understand it. Maybe it's the air down at the brush factory, the fumes from the celluloid production. I don't know. I can't seem to shake this cough. Once I stop coughing I'm fine. Give me a moment."

Maggie interceded, fussing, fretful, giving away her frustration. "He works too hard," she told her grown-up children, talking as though Oscar weren't there. "He's just working himself to death. Everything's all right for a few weeks and then the coughing starts. I wish he didn't have to walk so far to get to work. I wish he would take the trolley. We can certainly afford it. Business has been very good lately. Money's not a problem for us these days."

Oscar replied testily, "Oh please. I enjoy the walking. It gives me time to wake up in the morning before I get to work and time to think on the way home in the evening."

James spoke up, his voice showing his concern. "Dad, if you took the trolley you wouldn't be so tired all the time. You wouldn't be so susceptible to little things like this cough. You're not a common day laborer without the means to pay the fare. You should ride the trolley."

Oscar pulled in his chin and folded his arms across his chest. For a moment he rocked, still regaining his breath. "Ah, what do you mean about common day laborers? There's no difference between me and the other boys down at the brush factory. I'm their boss but I still make brushes, too. I enjoy turning out a good brush as much now as ever. I'm a brushmaker. That's who I am. It's what I do for a living."

James answered patiently, "That air in the celluloid building. It's not good for you. You could get a decent job. You could breathe fresh air. That's what you should do."

Now Oscar spoke angrily. "I have a decent job! Don't tell me what to do. I'm a brushmaker. I'm proud of my work. Proud of the things I make. People see my specialty brushes and they say I'm an artisan, an artist. I might not have a fancy job like you do down at the bank, Jimmy. Or like your engineering job, Gene. I'm proud of both of you and of the work you both do. But brushmaking suits me just fine."

Gene sat quietly, as was his way, watching his family, contemplating, considering what he should say. Finally he spoke, appeasing his father, sorting it out with his brother. "You're a fine craftsman, Dad. We're all proud of what you've done and how much you've accomplished. But maybe the walk to work each day is becoming too much. How long does it take you?"

"Maybe an hour, maybe a bit more when I'm coughing like this. Sometimes I have to stop and catch my breath in Vailsburg Park about halfway home. The whole walk is about three miles. I was walking that far to work when we were back in Lansingburgh. It's not a problem."

Gene nodded and continued. "I may be able to help," he said. "We're laying out some new streets, new neighborhoods up in Vailsburg, not far at all from your factory. I know a builder who'll be putting in new homes up there, fine new big houses with decent size yards. You could get one of the first houses he builds. Would you like me to talk to him for you?"

"Oh, I couldn't afford a brand new house. And with only Carrie still living here we have plenty of room."

Money was James' business. He was two steps ahead of Gene and Oscar. "How much would one of these new houses cost?" he asked his brother.

Gene leaned in toward James and Oscar. He knew what was involved with the houses being built in the new neighborhoods he surveyed. He was happy to offer his father his advice. "Five thousand dollars. Maybe a bit more depending on the house and the lot size."

"There you go," said Oscar. "It's too expensive. Your mother and I are comfortable here. We can manage the rent here just fine. We have some savings. And we have some small investments thanks to you, Jimmy. But I couldn't afford to spend more than three, maybe four-thousand dollars for a new house. And we don't need a bigger house anyway."

"That's not a problem Dad," answered James. "I could help you find a mortgage with a good rate. I know some people."

"What's a mortgage?" Oscar was intrigued. James had helped him with several other banking transactions. This might turn out to be another of James clever business ideas.

"You put as much money as you can afford into buying the new house, and the bank loans you the rest. Instead of paying rent here for this little house, you would spend your money paying off your loan from the bank. Every month instead of throwing away rent money, you'd be a little closer to owning the house. You could buy a much better house than this little one if I helped you find a mortgage. You could live in a better neighborhood. Vailsburg is a good place to be. A better class of people lives out there than here in Newark."

"There's nothing wrong with this house or with our neighbors," Oscar insisted, but the new mortgage idea was intriguing.

Carrie was excited. "A new house with a bigger yard! I could put in a garden and grow flowers."

"And maybe some vegetables too," Maggie added. "And Oscar my dear, you wouldn't wear yourself out having such a long walk to work each day."

"Oh, all right." Oscar conceded the fight. Maggie and all three of his children were committed to this sudden idea of a new house. He felt trapped but he knew when to let them have their way. "Jimmy if you could look into one of those mortgage things for me. And Gene, see what you can do about talking with that builder friend of yours."

*****

Their new house was nearly complete, the mortgage was set, and Oscar, Maggie, and Carrie planned to move to Vailsburg early in November. Oscar's health was still an issue.

"It's terrible," he admitted to Maggie one evening late in August, sitting in the kitchen of their old Newark house. "This should be the best time of our lives, but look at me. My hands are stiff all the time, and I just can't shake this cough. I can't make a decent brush with my hands like this. And they shake when I'm coughing."

"You'll be fine once we move. Our new house will be wonderful. And your walk to work will be just a few minutes each way."

"Mr. Hyatt spoke with me this morning. He's taken note of my lack of production over the last few months."

"He's a good man. He's always treated you well. He'll look out for you now."

"Maybe. I don't know. He sees me more as a manager than as a brushmaker. If I had to count on brushmaking, my job would be a concern. Mr. Hyatt talked with me a week ago about only working a few hours a week to manage the brush production. With fewer hours my wage might be cut."

Maggie nodded thoughtfully. "But we'll be fine," she said. "We've been putting money aside every week for years. We have our savings."

"When we buy that big new house, we'll have less money saved than before. We've already put an awful lot of money into it. Jimmy has us set up with that bank in Newark for this mortgage thing. They'll own about half of that house. If we can't pay that mortgage each month we could lose everything. I have to keep my hours up at the brushmaking factory."

"Do we have any options if Mr. Hyatt does cut your hours?"

"I don't know. I've worked my whole life, and now in a couple of months we'll be moving into a beautiful big house. But we'll have no money." Oscar tried to act calm, but his face showed his anxiety. He shook his head.

Maggie took his hand, leaning toward him, reassuring him. "What about your time in your regiment in the war? They have pensions for old soldiers, don't they?"

"Veterans, not old soldiers. And I'm not that old. I'm only fifty-four."

"But your cough and your hands. You were in the war. If there's money available for men like you, it would be all right to take it."

"I don't know. I work for a living. I don't need to accept charity."

"It's not charity. It's them paying you back for what you did during the war. I believe they do have money for disabled veterans of the war. One of my friends at church talked about it."

"I suppose. But I'm not disabled. As long as I can keep working I won't need it. If Mr. Hyatt does cut my hours, I'll check into it."

*****

Two weeks later Mr. Hyatt called Oscar over from the adjoining brush factory to his office in the main celluloid factory building. He directed Oscar to a chair and closed the door. "How are you feeling?" he began.

"Fine, Mr. Hyatt. Things are going well." Oscar stifled the tickle in his throat, willing himself not to cough. He wiped his nose quickly on his white, cotton handkerchief.

"Your men tell me you're still coughing a lot."

Oscar cleared his throat. "I suppose. It's not a problem. I still turn out some truly fine brushes."

"Yes, you do. Your craftsmanship is always exceptional. I do note that you can't make as many as you did a few years ago. Your hands are a bit clumsy. They seem to give you some trouble. But I'm paying you to manage the production of the brushes more than to make the brushes yourself. You're a good man, Oscar. We've built that brushmaking business together. But I need to make a change. I want you to continue working for me but just three days a week as a manager. I want you to come in Monday to set up the week's work, and then stop by again for a few hours on Wednesday to see how things are going. Friday you would come in one more time to wrap up the week's work, to take inventory and count our production."

Oscar shifted in his wood chair. He looked away from Hyatt, inspecting the wide top of his boss's rock maple desk. "That's what I do now. But I also make brushes on Tuesday and Thursday and when I have time on the other three days. I could still do that."

Mr. Hyatt was sensitive to Oscar's plight. They had become friends in the years since their first meeting on the street in Waterford outside the Van Kleeck's factory. But he knew it was time for Oscar to step back, to walk away from the brushmaking. He spoke with compassion. "It's time to let that go, Oscar. I want you to hire and train an apprentice. I want you to get a new brushmaker ready to take on that work. I'll need to take back some of your hours to pay the new brushmaker, but I'll increase your hourly pay rate. It will still work out to a bit of a pay cut. Will you be all right with that? I know you're buying a new house."

"Yes sir, I'll be moving up here to Vailsburg in a couple of months. I don't know what I'll do to afford it if my pay goes down."

"I've seen your new neighborhood. That will be a pretty nice place to live and a short walk to work, less than a mile."

"There is that. As long as I do have a job to come to."

"You'll still have work Oscar. Just not as many hours."

"Or as much income."

"We've been through a lot together, building this business. And personally, we've seen each other through some hard times. Are you going to be all right?"

Oscar remembered little Edna. He thought of how Hyatt had looked out for him through those dark days. And now he saw Mr. Hyatt's concern. "It's a business decision he has to make," Oscar thought. "But it's my livelihood he's taking away."

"I don't know," Oscar answered. "There is a disabled veteran's pension out there. I fought in the civil war. I might see if I could get that."

"That's good." Hyatt felt relief that Oscar had a way to maintain his income without full-time work in the brush factory. "Check into that. Let me know. And we'll bring in an apprentice to pick up some of your work. You can teach him your trade. I'd like you to start your new schedule by the end of the month."

They shook hands. Oscar walked away feeling like a part of his life was gone. He told the boys in the factory his news. They nodded, clapped him on the back, and wished him well. One of them mentioned that his nephew, an Irish kid who had just arrived in New York, was looking for work. He could learn to make brushes. Oscar told him to bring the boy by the factory for a talk.

He passed the remaining hours of the workday in a daze, tinkering with brushes, trimming the bristles absent-mindedly. At quitting time, he began the long walk home alone. Just like that he was no longer a brushmaker. It had been his livelihood since he was fourteen years old. Forty years. It was over.

Maggie knew things weren't right as soon as he came in. His head was down, his body sagging. When he looked up and met her eyes, he started to cry. She rushed to him and took his hands. "Oh, Oscar. What's happened?"

"I had that talk with Mr. Hyatt this afternoon. He called me in just like I was afraid he would. He's cutting my hours and having me give up the brushmaking. He wants me to manage the business and train a new apprentice. It's over."

"You'll still be managing the work?"

"Yes, but just three days a week. And training a new brushmaker to take my place. No matter how fast the new man learns brushmaking, he can't be as good at it as I am. I've been doing this my whole life."

"Oh, my dear Oscar. How could Mr. Hyatt do this to you after how you've built that business for him?"

"He's a business man. He's a friend but when it's all said and done, he's running a business, trying to make money."

"I know, but didn't he realize what it would do to you? He knows about our new house."

"Yes. I honestly think he believes that with the disability veterans' pension we'll be all right. And maybe we will. But it's not just the money. What he doesn't understand is that brushmaking is what I love to do. It's my life he's taking away more than my livelihood and my income."

"You need to get across town and talk to the people at the veterans' affairs office about that pension."

"I can't. Not yet anyway. I have to go back to work tomorrow and meet the new man, the apprentice. I'll still work my regular hours for several more weeks."

"Well, the first day you're out of work you'll go down to the veteran's office."

Oscar nodded solemnly. Without saying another word, he walked out the kitchen door and up the stairs. He lay on the bed with his eyes closed, his mind blank until Maggie called him to dinner.

*****

Two weeks later, on a Tuesday afternoon, Oscar sat across the desk from a clerk on the second floor of the veteran's affairs office in Newark. The clerk took a form out of a drawer in his blonde oak desk. He straightened the form, aligning its edge with the front of the desk. He looked up at Oscar and took out his fountain pen.

"I come down to Newark from Trenton one week each month to work with disabled veterans," he explained. "Now, you need a disability pension? You can't work anymore?"

Oscar nodded, his face expressionless. He recited, "My hours have been cut way back. I was a brushmaker at the Celluloid Manufacturing factory a few miles out toward Orange. They have me managing the business now, not making brushes any more. My hours have been cut in half."

"I thought these celluloid companies were making a good profit. Why did they cut your hours?"

"I'm sick. I've got rheumatism and my hands are too stiff to make the brushes. And I've got this issue with my head. I'm always congested, my nose won't stop running, and I cough a lot. Maybe it's due to the air in the celluloid factory. I don't know, but I can't work on the brushes when I'm coughing."

The clerk nodded. "Ah yes. The doctors call it catarrh. It's a chronic inflammation of the mucous membranes. A lot of the celluloid workers suffer from it. We see a lot of disability claims due to catarrh. But you said you'll still be working a few hours?"

"Yes. About half the hours I used to work. My wages are going way down."

The clerk nodded. "All right, then. Here's what we can do for you."

He turned the form to face Oscar and pointed to lines with his fountain pen. "You need to fill out this form. List 'Rheumatism and Catarrh in the head' right here where it asks what your disability is. And give me your address and your old regiment. We can get you started with a partial disability pension in a few weeks. If you ever lose your job completely you'll have to come in and fill out the form again to get the full pension."

The clerk tapped the form twice and offered Oscar the pen. "Make two copies if you could," he instructed. "One copy for me and the veteran's office and one to keep for your records."

Oscar took the forms and began to write. He felt as though he was signing away everything in his past. He was a brushmaker. He wrote on the form that he was a brushmaker, but he knew it was no longer true. All he could think was that now he wasn't able to do the work that had defined him since he was a boy.

When he finished with the form he handed it to the clerk. "You should come back in about two weeks, Mr. McMurray," said the clerk, scanning the form quickly. "We'll have your first disability payment in cash at that time. After that you'll be coming in to collect your money twice a year."

Without a word, Oscar shook the clerk's hand. He turned, went down the stairs and out the door of the office building. Back on the street, Oscar caught the trolley and rode home. He walked in the front door, through the house to the kitchen and sat at the table. Maggie came and sat with him. "It's over," he said. "I'm on the pension."

Two months later Oscar, Maggie, and Carrie moved to the vast new house set on a double lot on Richelieu Terrace in Vailsburg. They had more space than in any house where they had ever lived. Their furniture, even the piano, hardly filled the rooms. Regardless of the openness and brightness of the big new rooms, Oscar was morose, sitting idly at the kitchen table on the days when he wasn't at the factory.

Then one sunny morning, looking around at his fine new house, he began to smile. It was the nicest house he had ever lived in, as beautiful as the house where Maggie had lived with her family before she and Oscar were married.

There was even indoor plumbing. And his walk to and from work, on the days he went, was the shortest since he was a boy, back in the early days when he made brushes in the small shop behind his house in Lansingburgh. Slowly, he began to admit that his life had turned out well.

The Stereoscope

AS I WORK AT my father's old writing table, I look to my right and see the Teachout Family Bible, its' mass taking up half the space on a low bookshelf. On the shelf above is a stack of old books that includes the Doré *Idylls of the King*, my grandfather's second grade primer signed James H. McMurray, and the book that began my search, *The Flowers Personified*. These books have all played a part in the development of this story. I referred to them often. My research is almost finished. I think I finally know my ancestors.

On my left is my grandfather MacMurray's maple secretary desk, a tall piece of furniture with a fold-out desk top and glass-paned doors behind which I have stored a number of old family heirlooms. The secretary was left to me by my grandmother MacMurray. It sat in a basement with the drawers taped shut when I first got it. After several years I had the time and the money to refurbish it. When I was preparing the secretary to be restored, I discovered several items had been left inside the drawers by my grandparents, James and Grace. These things meant little to me at the time, but now that I've learned so much of the McMurray family story, I understand their significance. There were several of Oscar's brushes, of course, and two straight razors, one of them the old ivory-handled razor carved with the figure of a nude woman. I also found some pieces of ancient Navajo pottery which my mother might have acquired on her tour of the west when she was a teenager.

One of the artifacts in the secretary was particularly notable because it gave me new insight into the lives of Oscar and Maggie. Behind the glass-paned doors was an antiquity I had acquired and put aside without much thought until now. It's a stereoscope, a device popular in the late 1800s made from a design originally perfected by Oliver Wendell Holmes. A stereoscope has two offset lenses mounted in a wooden box sculpted to wrap around a user's face. There are cards to set on a rack in front of the lenses and view with the stereoscope, each card with two nearly identical photos of the same subject, taken from slightly different angles. When you hold the device to your eyes and look through it at a card, the stereoscope tricks your brain into seeing the image in three-dimensions. The stereoscope was a common novelty at the beginning of the twentieth century. In later years, the stereoscope was replaced by a plastic viewer called a View-Master with a cardboard disk of a dozen paired photographs for viewing. Both are relics now sometimes found in antique stores. Every few years there have been improvements in this three-dimensional illusion concept. Today we marvel at virtual reality technology.

My mother put the stereoscope and a stack of viewing cards in a yard sale in the 1980s. My mother-in-law bought it, telling my wife, "Peter likes history and old things. He should have this. He'll enjoy it."

I thought it was interesting and kept it, putting it in the old secretary along with some of the other old things I had acquired from my mother. But I never really looked through the old cards that came with it. Recently, inspired by my quest to learn about my family, I pulled out the stereoscope and sorted through the cards. Nearly half the stereoscope cards were from the 1904 Louisiana Purchase Exposition, the St. Louis World's Fair. These included pictures of exhibits at the fair and tourist scenes of Paris and Rome. There were shots of the White House, of Mount Vernon, of the Royal Palaces in Berlin and Fontainebleau and the Kremlin. I found four photographs of Teddy Roosevelt and his Rough Riders from the Spanish American War. And among all of these world-famous landmarks and historically notable pictures there were seven scenes of Waterford, New York, Maggie's home town. Maybe these stereoscope cards, like many of the other old family keepsakes, fit into the puzzle of who my ancestors are.

Now I wonder if Oscar and Maggie made a trip to the St. Louis World's Fair in 1904. I have no evidence that they did except the stereoscope and all those cards from the fair. But why not believe they went to the fair in St. Louis? How else could they have acquired the cards?

If they did, they would have probably taken a train; it's a long way to travel from New Jersey. While they were there, they would have seen many samples of the magnificent future everyone imagined at the beginning of the twentieth century. This exposition was where the world got its first look at new wonders like electricity, "autocars," and Alexander Graham Bell's radio telephone. The turn of the century was a time of innovation, entrepreneurship, and invention as richly filled with changes as any era before or since.

The fair offered a cash prize for anyone who could build a contraption able to fly over a looping measured course at a speed of fifteen miles an hour. No one claimed the prize, though a dirigible was there in St. Louis and tried. The Wright brothers' flight at Kitty Hawk had occurred just months before the St. Louis Fair, but the brothers didn't attend the fair and try for the prize since they were working on their airplanes in Ohio and North Carolina at the time.

It was a thrilling, evolving world in which Oscar and Maggie and their children lived. What might they have thought of St. Louis and all these wonderful new things?

28

1904: The Full Pension

MAY IN THE FARMLAND and rolling countryside of central New Jersey offered an idyllic setting for Eugene's wedding. Springtime turned the mood optimistic. The world was filled with buds, flowers, sunshine, and bird-song.

Oscar steered his horse-drawn carriage off the cobblestone streets of the cities of Newark and Vailsburg, out into the farmland, along the wide, packed-dirt roadway, past the orchards and horse farms, into the country to the west. Maggie rode in the seat next to him, a bonnet protecting her hair from the breeze, a light cloak covering her finest dress. James and Carrie shared the second seat. It was thirty miles to Germantown in western New Jersey. It took more than two hours to get to Eugene's wedding.

Mabel was a pretty girl, and Eugene was absolutely enthralled with her. From the moment she entered the church sanctuary and started down the aisle on her father's arm, Gene couldn't take his eyes off her. Maggie leaned to Oscar and whispered, "Look at him. He's so much in love with her."

Oscar whispered back, his breath in Maggie's thick curls of white hair. "It reminds me of us when we got married. I was the same way."

Maggie squeezed his hand. "You still are," she whispered. They settled back in the pew, relaxed and satisfied as they watched their oldest son become the first of their children to marry.

After the wedding, the guests and the newlyweds walked the short distance down the street from the church to an old inn for a reception and dinner. Mabel and Gene approached Oscar and Maggie. "Congratulations," Oscar said to his son clasping his hand and clapping him on the shoulder. "You've found a good woman with Mabel."

"Yes, I have." Gene pulled her to him, an arm around her waist. Mabel beamed, leaning against him, her hand on the front of his waistcoat, displaying the diamond ring he had bought for her.

"I'm sure you'll both be very happy," Maggie added, kissing each of them lightly on their cheeks.

"I know we will be." Mabel held Gene close. "He's such a refined gentleman, a man of culture, and he has a great job with Sawyer. How could we not be happy?"

James stood by, pleased with his big brother's joy. This was right for Gene. James felt no need to distract himself from his career to pursue life with a woman. But he loved the way Gene looked with Mabel.

Carrie too, was thrilled for her oldest brother and for Mabel. She clasped her hands happily in front of her as she watched the two of them, so bewitched, so much in love with each other, so close. They were like a prince and princess in a fairy tale.

Late in the afternoon, Oscar gathered Maggie, James, and Carrie for the carriage ride back to Vailsburg. James took the reins before they started, aware that his father was fatigued. Carrie sat beside her brother on the front seat. The horse trotted along, its hoof beats a hypnotizing rhythm for the tired passengers. Oscar dozed, leaning against Maggie in the back seat. He woke as they began to approach Newark, jostled by the cobblestone pavement and the noises of the carriage traffic around them.

"Where are we?" he asked, looking around.

"Almost home," James announced, concentrating on the road.

Carrie turned to look over her shoulder at her parents. "It was a wonderful day," she said. "And Gene will be settling back here in Newark with Mabel in a few days."

Maggie nodded. "That will be nice. We can still have them come by our house for Sunday dinner. And we'll see them at church too."

"I expect. They're married now but it will still be the same for all of us." Carrie sat back, pleased with how things were.

Oscar leaned forward to the front seat. "What about you two?" he asked. "Should we expect either of you to be getting married soon?"

Carrie looked at James. He took a quick look back at his sister and grinned. It was a question they had expected, laughing about it together. "I don't know," he said. "I'm so busy at work I don't really have the time for courting a young lady. And I haven't met anyone special anyway."

Maggie pushed him lightly on the shoulder. "Oh, Jimmy, there are plenty of fine young women around. I see several in church on Sunday. I see them looking at you. They know what an eligible young man you are. Open your eyes."

James chuckled quietly. "I don't know. The time will come I expect. But not now."

Oscar turned to Carrie. "How about you, young lady? Any thoughts about any of the young men you know?

"Oh, Daddy. I don't think so. I'll be turning thirty-six in a couple of days. If a man hasn't come courting yet I doubt he ever will."

Maggie turned a stern look on her daughter. "There's plenty of time for both of you. James, you'll find a young woman when you're ready. And Carrie, perhaps if you let the men know you were interested. Perhaps if they saw that you can cook and take care of a man's home, a man might show an interest. You're an attractive lady. But they have to know you're available. You could be having a day just like Gene and Mabel if you'd let it happen."

"I'll be just fine Momma. I'm happy staying at home with you and Daddy."

*****

Maggie bustled from the kitchen to the dining room. "Help me set the table, Carrie. James will be here soon. And Gene and Mabel will be along as well. This is the first time they'll all be joining us for Sunday dinner since they got married."

Carrie scooped up the dark wooden box Oscar had made to store the silver flatware. She carried it to the dining room where Maggie was floating a white table cloth across their new dining table.

"Don't forget the napkins," Maggie reminded Carrie, noting that Carrie was setting the silverware out without the linen napkins.

"Yes, Momma." Carrie sighed, collected the napkins from the sideboard and reset the table with the white linen napkins beneath the forks at each place.

James arrived several minutes later with Gene and Mabel right behind him. They gathered in the parlor with Oscar and Carrie, on the new sofas and wingback arm chairs. Light streamed in through the big bay window. It was the first time Oscar was able to furnish a house like Maggie's family home back in Waterford. Accepting the offer to move to New Jersey and start the celluloid brush business had been a rewarding decision for him. Even now, with his partial pension he was doing well in spite of the limited work days and pay. He looked around at his family and his big comfortable home on Richelieu Terrace, proud of what he had accomplished.

Maggie carried in a metal-rimmed wooden tray with six tall glasses of tea. Chips of ice, like wet crystals, floated in each glass, catching the sunlight. With Carrie's help, Maggie distributed the drinks to Oscar and her children.

Oscar raised his tea glass. "To the newlyweds!"

"To the newlyweds!" the family shouted.

"Thank you." Gene basked in the warmth of his family.

Mabel sipped her tea happily and grinned, bubbling with the ongoing excitement of her big day. "We brought you the leftover programs from the wedding," she said. "We thought you might each want one as a keepsake in case you didn't bring one home with you."

"I've already got one," said Maggie. "But thank you. I've got a good place to keep things like this. With two, I can keep one program out to look at and store the second one away with my other keepsakes."

"We've got our wedding portrait here too," said Gene, handing his mother a dark photograph in a narrow frame. "And we brought the guest book. We thought you all might like to look through it and see how many of our family and friends were able to be there."

Mabel continued, "I know that Germantown is a bit of a journey from here, but that's where I grew up. It's where my family still lives and where my church is. I was very happy so many people were able to come all that way out to my hometown for the wedding."

Maggie looked at the framed portrait of Eugene and Mabel. Then she set it up on a small table next to her chair for everyone to see. Oscar reached for the guest book, but James stretched out and took it. He thumbed through it. When he was finished he set it on a side table out of Oscar's reach. Maggie picked up the guest book. She opened it and began to look through the pages. Suddenly she paused, her face grim. She looked up at James. She handed the opened book to Oscar. James stared off at a painting on the wall, refusing to make eye contact with his parents.

Oscar looked at the guest book, at the page opened where Maggie had handed it to him. He froze. "James! What is this?"

James looked back at his father placidly. "What's what, Dad?"

"You know what. You signed yourself here on the book as James H. MacMurray. Not McMurray. I understand that the Prudential has you on their payroll with your name misspelled. My name. Our name. And you've left it like that even though it's wrong. But this is you writing it yourself, spelled wrong right here in Gene and Mabel's guest book."

James smiled and gave a light wave of his hand, dismissive of the problem. "It's nothing Dad. MacMurray. McMurray. Who cares. It's nothing."

Maggie looked at her children. Carrie was amused, giggling quietly behind her hands as she watched the fight unfold. Gene was looking sternly at his little brother. Mabel seemed confused by the debate that was exploding in her new family.

"Oh, Daddy," said Carrie. "Sometimes James spells his name differently. It's not a problem."

"It most certainly *is* a problem!" Oscar was red in the face. "We're McMurrays. It's our name. It's who we are. You can't change your name." The final comment was emphasized with an arthritic finger pointed at James, jabbing on each word.

"Okay. Okay, Dad, settle down. Sometimes I spell it with an a. I believe we're Scottish and that's a Scottish spelling. I know we couldn't be Irish. We're not like the Irish. We aren't Catholic—we're Methodist. We aren't like those common day laborers, coming home after a hard day working in some factory, sitting on the front stoop in our undershirt with a bottle of dark beer in our hand. That's how the Irish are. We're not like that. We're more refined. I mean, look at this house and the way we live. The Irish don't live like this. So I add the letter a, and we're Scottish. It's not a big problem, is it?"

Oscar pointed at his son again, the finger with the swollen knuckles wagging. "Yes! It absolutely is a problem! Don't forget where you come from. Don't forget who you are. I'm of Irish descent. We all are. You can't just go and change that. Take pride in who you are."

"I'm not Irish. Or Scottish," said Mabel, missing Oscar's point. "I'm an Apgar. My family is German."

"Just as bad as the Irish," argued James. "But they're a different kind of bad. The Huns, always at war over there in Europe."

Mabel was taken aback by James' words. Gene saw it and reached for her hand. Mabel fought back against James' insult, pushing her new husband's hand away. "We're not like that. My family came over to New York more than a century ago. I think after a generation or two we're all Americans anyway."

"So there," said Carrie, palms out, smiling at her brothers. "We've all been in this country for several generations too. So, we're all Americans. It's settled." For her, the debate was over.

"Of Irish descent," insisted Oscar. "And I don't drink beer when I come home, but there's nothing wrong with working in a factory."

"They're common. They're day laborers. You work with them. You see them, Dad. We're not at all like them."

"We're more like them than you might imagine. I've done well with my work. I manage them. I know them, and they're good men. Hard-working, skilled, talented men. Responsible men with families. Many of them are Catholic, but they're pious. They just attend a different church. Some of the things they do might not be what I choose to do, but that's their choice."

Maggie nodded. "Drinking alcoholic beverages is wrong. It's not the way we live, but they are good people, the Irish. Devout, even if they are of a different faith. Remember who you are, James. Enough of this masquerade as a Scot."

James became angry, his face flushed, suddenly shouting. "I don't want anyone thinking I'm Irish. It might not be a problem for you, but it is for me. Do you really imagine that I would have gone as far with Prudential if they knew I was of Irish descent? Of course not. And Dad, maybe you would have done better with your job at the Hyatts' factory if they didn't know you were Irish."

Oscar shouted, "You have a problem with what I do for a living? What I've done?" He started to stand and took a short step toward James. Then he froze, red in the face again and gasping for breath. He staggered backward a step and fell back into his chair. His breath wheezed. He sucked for air, his shoulders heaving. He leaned over, his head between his knees fighting to get his breath back. His family sat in silence watching him, waiting for him to recover. Maggie leaned to him, rubbing his back gently, coaxing him to breathe.

"Oscar, sweetheart. Relax. Take a deep breath. Get your breath back."

She looked across at James. He sat stunned in his chair, aghast, watching his father fighting for air.

"I didn't mean to... I didn't know it would upset him so."

Quietly, her voice contained, though angry, Maggie addressed him. "Jimmy, perhaps you should leave today. Come back for dinner next Sunday when your dad has gotten himself together. And don't bring this Irish issue up again." She allowed no debate.

"Yes, Mother." He stood and tiptoed out of the house.

Dinner that day was awkward. Conversation was subdued, mostly about Gene and Mabel's wedding and their new home together. Nobody came back to the Scottish-Irish debate though James' empty place at the table kept it at the front of everyone's mind.

He returned for Sunday dinner a week later. Conversation with his family was jovial. Gene and Mabel had taken the wedding guest book home with them a week earlier. It was as though nothing had happened. Nobody talked about the Scottish name again, but nobody forgot about it.

*****

Mr. Hyatt sat with Oscar at his worktable in the brush factory. Warm, late summer sun caught the fine celluloid dust in the factory air, the sunbeams seeming as substantial as the translucent polished brush handles. Fiinished new brushes were stacked, sometimes boxed, on the tabletops. The big room was orderly, the floor swept, the twenty-five work tables perfectly aligned like ranks of well-trained soldiers. All the brushmakers except Oscar had left for the day.

"Look at this place," Hyatt said. "Think about what you've built here, Oscar. We're turning out brushes at a rate that can match any other brush factory in the country."

"Better quality than most, too," Oscar said proudly. "People look for our products in stores."

"They certainly do. You've done this. You have a lot to look back on and be proud." Hyatt clapped Oscar lightly on the shoulder.

Oscar nodded. Where was this conversation going, he wondered? Hyatt was a friend, but he rarely came to the brush factory just to chat. They usually met at his office in the big celluloid factory next door.

"Thank you, Mr. Hyatt." Oscar watched his boss carefully.

"You're welcome. And thank you for building this business. It's been almost twenty years of hard work from you and your boys. I'd like to have a small celebration at the end of the workday in a week or so. I'll provide a light meal and some cold drinks. I think it would be a good time they'd all enjoy."

Oscar nodded again. "Yes, that would be very nice."

Hyatt's tone changed. He spoke slowly, deliberately. "And I think it's time we made a change again, Oscar. You still struggle at times here at work. I worry about you. I'd like you to step back again. It's best for your health. You're still on only a partial pension? Do you think you could go on the full pension?"

Oscar looked around the wide factory space. He saw the work benches, each stacked with the day's production, ready to be shipped. He did a quick tally of the brushes in his head. He loved the look and the feel of a well-made brush. The deftly crafted handle, amber plastic polished smooth and contoured to fit a person's hand. The flat surface of the rough bristles and the way they felt if you dragged your finger across them. He would miss all this.

He knew what was coming—Hyatt was letting him go. The after-work festivities would be to celebrate the thriving business he had built but also to tell him good-bye.

*****

Once again Oscar sat at the desk in the veteran's affairs office in Newark. The clerk returned from a file cabinet carrying a folder with a form in it. He pushed his narrow glasses back on the bridge of his nose and scanned the paper quickly. Then he spoke to Oscar, never taking his eyes off the form.

"Ah yes. Mr. McMurray. It says here that you began a partial disability pension in 1897. How are you doing?"

"You worked with me to fill out that form back then. Remember?"

"I can't say that I do. There are so many veterans I see each day, every year. But I see that you are a brushmaker and that you went on partial disability seven years ago."

"I remember you. So, you ask how I'm doing? Not well. The brush factory let me go. They said it was time."

"Your catarrh is worse? Your rheumatism?"

"I suppose." Oscar looked down at his hands, embarrassed to admit that he could no longer work. It felt like an affront to his manhood.

"That's not a concern. We'll fill out a new form and put you on a full disability pension. Everything will be just fine."

"No, it won't be fine. I've lost my job. I've lost my livelihood."

"You'll have a full pension. You'll still have a nice income. More than you've been receiving with the partial pension. You'll be fine." The clerk spoke with compassion, his hands out, hoping the man in front of him would understand how sensible the full pension was.

"I'll have money, but I won't have my brushmaking. Don't you see that?"

"You'll be fine. Let's just fill out the form."

The clerk handed a fountain pen and two fresh forms to Oscar. It only took Oscar two minutes to give the necessary details, and he was finished filling out the forms. As he had done seven years earlier, he made two copies, one for the veterans' office, one more for himself.

The clerk reviewed the new forms quickly. He placed one copy in a tray on his desk. Then he stood and gave Oscar his copy. Oscar folded it and put it in his coat pocket.

"Congratulations, Mr. McMurray. You're on a full pension. That's all there is to it. What are you going to do with all your new free time?"

"I don't know."

"Well I'm sure you'll find all sorts of things to do to occupy yourself now that you don't have to work." He extended his hand, expecting a handshake from Oscar.

192

Oscar nodded but said nothing. He stood, ignoring the clerk's outstretched hand, turned and walked down the stairs, out of the office. He began walking back up the long road to Vailsburg. He felt nothing. His mind was empty. He had no job, no future. He was a master craftsman, a brushmaker, but now he could no longer make brushes.

Part way back along South Orange Avenue to his home in Vailsburg he stopped and sat on a bench in Vailsburg Park. While he caught his breath, he thought about the busy work-day world he saw moving past him, the carriages, the wagons, and the trolleys. They passed in both directions, two endless streams hurrying to important destinations, carrying people, moving goods from factories to markets. For him there was no rush anymore. He had no place to go but home and nothing to do when he got there but sit. The world rolls on, he thought. But what can I do? It moves along without me now.

His destination was his home and Maggie. She was his north star, all that truly mattered, he told himself, but there would be nothing to occupy his mind or his hands whenever he got there, nothing he could say to Maggie. There was no need to hurry. He sat for an hour longer watching the traffic. Then, slowly, he stood and began to walk the rest of the way home.

He needed to put a good front on this for Maggie. He couldn't have her feeling his emptiness. Maybe he and Maggie could take a vacation? Maybe they could go to that World's Fair out in St. Louis? Maybe the man at the pension office was right and he could do anything he wanted to do now that he had the time. The only thing he couldn't do was make brushes, but that was who he was, a master brushmaker. That was what he wanted to do.

"I'm home!" Oscar called as he came through the carved front door of their house. His voice was infused with a jovial, breezy, artificial enthusiasm.

"They took care of it? You're all set with the full pension?" Maggie came to him, wrapped her arms around him and kissed him, the best comfort he could imagine. She always knew what he needed most. He smothered himself in her hair.

"Yes, of course. We'll have enough money. Not to worry. What do you say we celebrate! Let's take a vacation. I've been thinking we might go out to that Louisiana Exposition in St. Louis, the World's Fair celebrating the centennial of the Louisiana Purchase. What do you say?"

Maggie beamed at her happy husband, leaning back in his arms. "It sounds like a marvelous idea! Could we take the train to get there?"

"I believe so. I've got some money tucked away. We'll find a nice hotel too."

Maggie kissed him again. "When do we leave?"

Oscar's Passing:
July 1907

MAGGIE SAT QUIETLY IN the parlor. She was dressed in her formal black dress, high necked, long-sleeved, the one she saved for funerals. It seemed there was always a friend from the church, one of the older ladies passing away. Maggie thought it was prudent to have a special dress for such occasions. Curiously she didn't feel the summer heat today, even in the long black mourning dress. She felt chilled.

She closed her eyes. Her hands were folded loosely in her lap. Her mind was a blank wall of whiteness. That was by choice; she had to keep the chaotic thoughts, the frantic nagging ones, her fears and her despair to herself. The only way she had coped this past week was by self-control, keeping it all inside. She had held it together through the funeral and the interment. Now she was home, asking her children to give her some time with her thoughts. She was alone though she was glad they were nearby, down the hall together in the kitchen.

Maggie tallied the years in her head. They had met forty-six years ago in the spring of 1861. They were married in April 1867. They were married more than forty years. Two months ago, she turned fifty-nine. She could hardly remember a time when Oscar wasn't there with her.

Now he was gone.

Maggie heard her children, all grown now in their thirties, talking as they sat around the kitchen table. She wanted to be strong for them, to have something to tell them, a consoling word she could say that would make it better. Wasn't that what a mother should do for her children even when they were adults? But what could she say? Oscar was gone. They had lost their father, and no words could change that.

She also knew they wanted to help her, to soothe her, to say something to lessen her grief. And she knew they couldn't and that they felt badly about their inadequacy. She wished she could say to them that she understood, and it was going to be all right. They all shared this grief. She remembered little Edna's passing, not that long ago. They had all survived that terrible time and they would get through this as well. Some people live long full lives. Others only survive a few months. Death is the inevitable, unavoidable end for all of us, she thought. Today, philosophy wouldn't help. Oscar was gone. That was all there was to say about it.

The church had been very good to her and the children. Reverend Dickison had been by the house to see her twice before the funeral, and his service and the interment were as nice as she could have hoped. Some of the ladies from church, her prayer circle and the Bible study group, had brought food to the house. She and her children had plenty to eat. But food couldn't fill the void she felt inside.

Maggie thought how foolish it was! Oscar had always suffered from indigestion. Ever since the war, things hadn't sat right with him. Maybe it was the illness he had endured when he was on the Mississippi River. Maybe that had damaged his digestive system. Maybe it was due to his chronic head colds, his catarrh, his difficulty breathing. Maybe it was the bad air in the celluloid factory. It didn't matter.

When it happened, it was so sudden. One day they were enjoying a dinner, just the two of them, and the next day Oscar was bent over with terrible pains in his stomach. "Intestinal Nephritic" the doctor called it, something to do with his intestines and his kidneys. The doctor gave him medicine for the pain, and Oscar slept. He woke late at night, moaning in the bed with her and then he stopped and seemed to sleep again, quiet but still restless. He was gone by morning. Just like dear little Edna, passing away in his sleep.

As he always did, James had taken charge of all the arrangements. Maggie knew that Gene and Carrie cared too, but it was James who took command in situations like this. He completed all the paperwork, made the plans for the funeral, and looked into Maggie's finances. James told her she would be able to live comfortably in their fine home on Richelieu Terrace for the rest of her life. Something about the pension and some insurance. There was more paperwork James would help her complete. But what did it matter? So she still had money. What could she do, how could she live without Oscar?

Maggie heard shouting from the kitchen, Gene raising his voice, taking on James. "You know how Dad felt about it. We're McMurrays. That's all there is to it. Leave it alone. He's dead now, but I think you should respect his wishes. I know I'll honor him that way."

Maggie heard James mumbling an answer. Carrie said something as well, the words blurred by the length of the hallway. It was the same discussion as it always was with James. "We're not Scottish, no matter how much James wants to pretend we are," Maggie thought. "I'm just too tired to fight about it today."

She leaned back, resting her head against the carved, black wooden crest on the back of the green upholstered chair and closed her eyes again. "The sun is shining," she thought. "It's a perfect July day today. The sun will likely be shining again tomorrow. Maybe I can start the rest of my life tomorrow. But not today. I'm just too tired."

She slept.

Afterword

WITH MY PARENTS AND my grandparents no longer living, the facts behind their stories are lost to me. I may never know the truth about all the heirlooms or have a full, factual narrative of my family heritage.

Things left in drawers of my grandfather James' old secretary, papers stuffed in a battered manila envelope beneath the guestroom bed, and the boxes I discovered in my mother's basement were filled with small clues to the MacMurray family history. Along with the stereoscope and other objects, there were the daguerreotypes of Oscar and Maggie that I now keep on the fold out top of the secretary desk. I turned and looked at their faces as I reconstructed my account of what their lives might have been like. I based my stories about them only slightly on my mother's accounts because her tales have proven to be so inaccurate. I grounded my story more on the information my research provided. I don't promise that my version of Oscar and Maggie's life together is true. What I know for sure is that mother's recollections weren't.

That may not be unusual. As this book developed, I discovered that family stories are frequently less than totally accurate. People who have reviewed chapters of this book have shared with me their own family secrets, the folklore and the fantasies that seem to be commonplace in many family traditions. It seems that it's not unusual for family stories to get embellished over time. The oral history of characters and events is fluid. Stories change after being retold many times. Some are total fabrications, like the romantic story about our Swedish spinning wheel. Others, like the life of Oscar's Uncle Albert, are deliberately hushed. These are stories of events that families are not proud of, black sheep that must be kept hidden.

The fundamental fabrication in the McMurray family history is the name change, switching our national heritage from Irish to Scottish. This, too, is common. The spelling of names doesn't seem to be as big a concern in many families as it has turned out to be in mine. Families know their names have been changed for a variety of reasons. They acknowledge it and laugh about it. What is unusual with the MacMurray name change is the denial, the lengths that my grandfather, and then my mother went to in order to convince themselves and the people they knew of our Scottish heritage. Re-writing the name on documents, creating the myth of our immigration from County Argyll in Scotland, developing the tale that Eugene changed his name to the Irish spelling so that his architectural firm could get contracts to build Catholic cathedrals, all of this was done to hide our true heritage. In the end, the revisions became too elaborate to be believed. Lies fall apart the more they are told.

Maybe I make too much of the name change, obvious as it now is. People have suggested I should have my DNA checked to confirm my nationality. It would probably tell me nothing more than that I'm Scotch/Irish, so what's the point? MacMurray or McMurray, we are who we are and the reality of Oscar's and Maggie's lives remains unchanged.

Regardless, the stories about Oscar and Maggie and their children fascinate me. Some of the stories my mother told me about them might be true. But I have discovered that many, like Oscar's imprisonment in Virginia during the Civil War, are nonsense. My version of Oscar and Maggie's life together is rooted in what I have learned during my travels to Lansingburgh and Vailsburg and other locales where my ancestors lived, by the hidden artifacts I found when my mother passed away, by my review of old family documents, and all that my internet research showed me.

There are common themes to family stories that form the basis for Oscar and Maggie's tale. Major events like weddings, births, and deaths create the framework. Men and women have been falling in love, marrying, and raising children for centuries. Men have also been going off to war for eons, and, for at least as long as there has been written history, women have been waiting anxiously at home for their men to return. Ask Penelope what it was like waiting all those years for Odysseus to return from Troy. It's no different when soldiers go off to fight today. Now, husbands wait for military wives as well.

Sometimes the soldiers don't return from a war and that becomes part of the family story. When they do come home, Post-Traumatic Stress Disorder may always have been too common. It seems it was for Uncle Stub. Only in recent years has this condition been acknowledged. But many veterans love to tell tales, sometimes true, sometimes fanciful, about their experiences in the military. Whether or not the soldiers go into combat they all go through an essential stage of life that changes their perspective. Debbie's father Merlin has his Navy stories. I still wish I knew more about my father's Uncle Miles. Soldiers remain soldiers for the rest of their lives.

People are defined by their work. They find their self-identity in their vocations and trades, even after they stop working. They take pride in what they do, and it is common for them to fear the loss of their jobs. To lose a job is for a person to lose not just their income, but their identity and their sense of self-worth. Having worked in human resources I know that people still feel these stresses today. I believe they always have and always will.

When work and the economy decline it is common for people to leave their homes and move to more hospitable economic environments to assure their families a good life. Centuries ago that might have meant the McMurrays' moving from Ireland to America. My wife Debbie's ancestors Olivia and Anders left Sweden for America, bringing that spinning wheel. Debbie's grandparents' family abandoned the prairie for Oregon during the dustbowl. Oscar's father headed west to the prairie possibly because economic conditions deteriorated in Lansingburgh. I know for certain that Oscar moved his family from Lansingburgh to Newark, and I assume it was so he could leave the failing economy of Lansingburgh to work in the emerging Celluloid brushmaking business, but I can't be sure.

I believe everyone wants to leave their mark on the world before they die, something that could tell future generations, "I was here." They might leave behind an heirloom, something they have created like Oscar's brushes. Their stories might also be their legacy. These heirlooms and stories should be preserved so that future generations understand who their ancestors were and what they accomplished. For me, writing this book has helped me fulfill that goal. And by reading this book you have done your part to perpetuate my legacy. You now know and remember me, my mother, my grandfather James, and Oscar and Maggie.

A person's legacy might be as simple as having children and sharing the family folklore with them. It may be natural that we want to leave these traces of ourselves behind, our family stories and the small changes we made in the world. We want to know that we made the world different because we lived. We want to be remembered. As I researched this book, I discovered many traces of Oscar and Maggie, brushes and books, daguerreotypes and old documents that were buried in boxes in my mom's house. If these traces were once lost or hidden, now they have been found. I have restored and preserved them.

In the beginning I knew little about my heritage because my mother had hidden so many facts from me and had changed the narrative too many times. I didn't know or understand anything about Oscar and Maggie. Now I do. They are real for me. I feel that I know them, and I sense their love, their struggles, and their fears. I believe that if their story lives, so do they. It's fiction but with a factual context. Whether or not it is the truth, my version of their legacy is now preserved. They are remembered.

Acknowledgments

I COULD NOT HAVE completed the journey of discovery that led to this book without many people helping me along the way. I should begin by thanking my mother. Even if her stories were so often inaccurate they gave me a placed to start. She also kept so many family heirlooms and artifacts, sometimes poorly preserved, but still in our family's possession.

I must also thank other relatives and friends for their insights into my family history. My father rarely talked about his family but his stories are part of my past. Some of my father-in-law Merlin Carr's stories are featured here. There are many more. I only scratch the surface of the many Merlin stories about his childhood in Portland Oregon, on the farm in South Dakota and from his days in the Navy.

Although I never received a response to my letter to a distant relative, Dorothy Karcher, her documents made a significant contribution to this book. She also investigated the McMurray family history and she shared her research and the documents she found with my mother. Now I have her notes.

My research included visits to some of the places Oscar and Maggie lived. I appreciate the time the staff at the Rensselaer County Historical Society gave to me. They shared insights into life in nineteenth century Lansingburgh and Waterford, New York, into the brushmaking business and into the civil war history of the region. They helped me find Oscar and Maggie's house, the birthplace of my grandfather James. I also value the attention I received from James Padgett, a Park Ranger at the Chatham Manor in Fredericksburg, Virginia. He tracked Stub's regiment, the New York 123rd and sent me a letter from that regiment describing their involvement in the fighting at Chancellorsville. He also reviewed my chapters about that battle and offered suggestions.

The internet provided more clues. My wife Debbie worked Ancestry.com and found a wealth of information about Oscar, Maggie, Sylvester and other relatives in this story. Google and Wikipedia provided additional information on a variety of topics, several Civil War regiments and battles, Van Kleeck's Brushmaking, Celluloid, J. Henry Theberath, the 1904 St. Louis World's Fair and more. What I learned from my Google searches was sometimes contradictory and needed additional study for corroboration. It is common knowledge that not everything we read on the internet is true. But then not everything we preserve in family stories is true either.

I can't call my stories finished until they have been reviewed by my two groups of writer friends. Among them are Tim Holland, Elizabeth Brown, Cindy Freeman, Cynthia Fridgen, Pat Ryther, Barbara McLennan, Dave Pistorese, Sharon Dillon, Sue Williamson, and Chris Pascale. They offered criticism, suggestions and support for every chapter of this book. It is much better because of their advice. Four other writer friends gave me valuable tips that enhanced the finished product. I depended on Brian Schulz, Ellen Smith, Liz Haskins, and Bob Archibald for their kind guidance.

Blue Fortune Publishing, my editor Narielle Living and the staff at Blue Fortune have made this book come to life. I am thankful to them for working with me.

Lastly, I thank my wife, Debbie. I have counted on her for much more than her internet research on Ancestry and other sites. I owe her thanks for her editorial critique of the whole book. She has corroborated Merlin's stories and her other family folktales. Above all, I have leaned on her for her emotional support as I worked through the hardest parts of what was at times a difficult personal journey. I could not have finished this book without her.

About the Author

As an author, Peter Stipe draws on his experiences in Human Resources Development in a variety of businesses. He holds a BA degree in History from Boston University and a Master's in Education from Tufts University. A New England resident for many years, he now lives and writes in Williamsburg, VA.

CPSIA information can be obtained
at www.ICGtesting.com
Printed in the USA
FFHW011635041119
55888132-61768FF